THE FIGURE IN CLAY

*Contemporary Sculpting Techniques
by Master Artists*

THE FIGURE IN CLAY
Contemporary Sculpting Techniques
by Master Artists

ARLEO
BOGER
BURNS
GONZÁLEZ
JECK
NOVAK
SMITH
TAKAMORI
WALSH

LARK BOOKS

A Division of Sterling Publishing Co., Inc.
New York

Editor: **Suzanne J. E. Tourtillott**

Art Director: **Dana M. Irwin**

Cover Designer: **Barbara Zaretsky**

Assistant Editor: **Nathalie Mornu**

Associate Art Director:
Shannon Yokeley

Assistant Art Director: **Lance Wille**

Editorial Assistance:
Delores Gosnell

Editorial Intern: **Janna Norton**

Page 5, Elaina Wendt, *Gift* (detail),
2002. Photo by artist

Page 98, by permission of the
Tacoma Art Museum

Acknowledgments

Nan Smith, with unswerving dedication to this book despite numerous deadlines, surgeries, and revisions, is an example of a true professional artist. She was my conduit to the world of figurative ceramic artists, and was able to entice some of the finest contemporary persons to be a part of it. Nan and eight other ceramists took time from their careers as lecturers, teachers, and artists to write their chapters and create the remarkable and challenging works shown herein, and for such labor I owe my deepest appreciation. These artists then invited still others, themselves among the most innovative of ceramic practitioners, to contribute gallery images of their own work; to them, too, I'm sincerely grateful.

And finally, without the superwomanly talents of my Lark teammate Nathalie Mornu, assistant editor, aided by Janna Norton, editorial intern, the myriad parts of this project could never have come together as they did; I applaud you.

Library of Congress Cataloging-in-Publication Data

Tourtillott, Suzanne J. E.
  The figure in clay : contemporary sculpting techniques by master artists / Suzanne J.E. Tourtillott.
    p. cm.
  ISBN 1-57990-611-7 (hardcover)
  1. Ceramic sculpture--Technique. 2. Human figure in art. I. Title.
  NK4235.T68 2005
  731'.82--dc22
                                   2004028210

10 9 8 7 6 5 4 3

Published by Lark Books, a division of
Sterling Publishing Co., Inc.
387 Park Avenue South, New York, NY 10016

© 2005, Lark Books

Distributed in Canada by Sterling Publishing,
c/o Canadian Manda Group, 165 Dufferin Street
Toronto, Ontario, Canada M6K 3H6

Distributed in the United Kingdom by GMC Distribution Services,
Castle Place, 166 High Street, Lewes, East Sussex, England BN7 1XU

Distributed in Australia by Capricorn Link (Australia) Pty Ltd.,
PO Box 704, Windsor, NSW 2756 Australia

If you have questions or comments about this book, please contact:
Lark Books, 67 Broadway, Asheville, NC 28801
(828) 253-0467

Manufactured in China

ISBN 13: 978-1-57990-611-5
ISBN 10: 1-57990-611-7

For information about custom editions, special sales, premium and corporate purchases, please contact Sterling Special Sales Department at 800-805-5489 or specialsales@sterlingpub.com.

Figures mirror and record the human experience, revealing aspects of both the inner and outer lives of those who made them.

—Michaelene Walsh

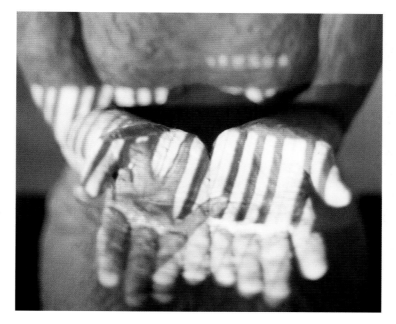

ARNEO
BOGER
BURNS
GONZÁLEZ
JECK
NOVAK
SMITH
TAKAMORI
WALSH

CONTENTS

Justin Novak, *Disfigurine (Competition)*, 2000
15 x 11 x 11 in. (38.1 x 27.9 x 27.9 cm)
Ceramic, glaze
PHOTO BY ARTIST. COURTESY NANCY MARGOLIS GALLERY

INTRODUCTION

Since that obscure moment in pre-history when innovative fingers first pinched metaphorical life into clay, no challenge in ceramic sculpture has inspired a greater range of response than representation of the human figure. From squat, goggle-eyed Jōmon creatures to brightly glazed Tang tomb guardians, molded terra cotta Tanagra goddesses, and Victorian faux-marble busts, the human body has been sculpted in a remarkable array of what seem to be intentionally different interpretations. An abundance of styles and techniques seems to have been forever at the ceramist's disposal. One naturally assumes that decisions have always been consciously made regarding ways of representing a subject known to us all so intimately.

This assumption, however, may be largely a consequence of our age, a period in which numerous exhibitions of historical objects and countless images of artifacts in books, magazines, and even digital media have made every moment from the past seem accessible at once. A similar condition exists regarding the objects produced by different cultures, which are often presented side by side in publications and exhibitions like goods at a multiethnic bazaar. The modern age, through its accumulation of information and images, has made possible a steady gaze down the length of history and across the breadth of cultures. Consequently, we recognize and even attribute value to the tremendous potential for variety in the simple act of fashioning a human figure in clay. Our times are characterized not only by our acceptance of representation through a multitude of techniques and styles but also by our encouragement of it.

Patti Warashina, *"A" Procession*, 1986
8 x 10 x 3 ft. (2.4 x 3 x 0.9 m)
Slip-cast and hand-built whiteware; electric fired,
cone 06; underglaze, glaze, acrylic sheet, wood
PHOTO BY ROGER SCHREIBER

In this regard, the sculptors featured in this book
are typically contemporary. Unlike their prede-
cessors of little more than a century ago, they
clearly do not feel bound—either by academic
formulas or by the weight of cultural tradition—to
a common mode of representing. They exempli-
fy a tendency in ceramic figural sculpture that
was already well established in the United States
by the late 1970s, when many of the greatest
names were emerging in what has since been
aptly called the New Ceramic Art. The visual dis-
tinctions between Robert Arneson's massive
portrait busts and Patti Warashina's miniature
slip-cast sprites could scarcely have been more
pronounced, nor could there have been a
greater contrast between Viola Frey's colossal,
craggy satires of figurines, Stephen DeStaebler's
haunting fragmentary bodies, and Richard
Shaw's meticulously crafted anthropomorphic
trompe l'oeil assemblages.

Robert Arneson, *Up Against It*, 1978
13 x 11 x 5 in. (33 x 27.9 x 12.7 cm)
Glazed ceramic
COLLECTION OF CONTEMPORARY MUSEUM, HONOLULU, HI;
GIFT OF PETER AND EILEEN NORTON. ART © ESTATE OF ROBERT
ARNESON/LICENSED BY VAGA, NEW YORK, NY. IMAGE COURTESY
OF GEORGE ADAMS GALLERY, NEW YORK.

The technical and stylistic diversity of the 1970s (what the art world at the time described as *pluralism*) has continued unabated into the present, creating the impression that virtually anything is possible in ceramic sculpture today. In a certain sense this may be true. Undoubtedly today's sculptor has a great deal more freedom to experiment with technique than was the case in centuries past. In 1877 the great modern artist Auguste Rodin found himself at the center of scandal when some mistakenly believed that his *Age of Bronze* had been cast from life, a violation of propriety that even Rodin would have despised. Exactly a hundred years later, the ceramic sculptor Howard Kottler managed to provoke the anger of purists in the ceramics community by casting sections of his work in hobby shop molds. Today few eyebrows are raised at the mold-made sculptures of ceramists such as Mark Burns and Nan Smith. Even the incorporation of found objects into ceramics, as in the sculptures of Arthur González, is no longer widely viewed as an offense.

The freedom enjoyed by contemporary ceramic sculptors is potentially misleading, however, since it seems to suggest that specific guidelines no longer exist for sculpture and that one can therefore work without concern for the standards of a period style. Diversity seems to have eliminated any shared sense of what ceramic sculpture should be and to have substituted for it only the encouragement that works be in some way unique. But this impression is not entirely accurate. Widespread acceptance in the art world has actually made artistic diversity the equivalent of our period style. In fact, diversity exercises an influence over art making that is every bit as conventional as that of traditional styles. The freedom to experiment with a variety of techniques and styles—some borrowed and some invented—does not, after all, imply that the sculptor is free of all responsibility. Acceptance of one's work by an audience still depends on fulfillment of certain expectations for what constitutes sculpture.

Precisely because so many techniques and styles are available for use by today's ceramic sculptor, choices about how to make one's work have become more important than ever. In the distant past, technique and style were often taken for granted, since the effectiveness of sculpture was rarely a consequence of its inventiveness. On the contrary, a certain degree of adherence to precedent was expected. Only with the advent of Modernism did originality become the crowning virtue in art. In the late 19th century, being modern and original meant participating in the development of new styles and techniques. Today the concept of artistic originality has become somewhat more complex. Skepticism about novelty has led many in the art world to redefine originality as less a matter of invention than of selection. Developing new techniques and styles is now less important than discovering creative ways of combining elements of already existing styles and techniques.

As the sculptors in this book demonstrate, this process of selection and combination can give rise to unique work. Some of these sculptors— Justin Novak, for instance—make obvious ref-

Mark Burns, *Old Queen Teapot*, 1998
24 x 22 x 10 in.
(61 x 55.9 x 25.4 cm)
Hand-built and slip-cast earthenware; electric fired, cone 03; commercial underglazes, glazes, cone 04; china paint, luster, cone 018; silk flowers
PHOTO BY ARTIST

erence to historical forms while using techniques with which those forms are not ordinarily associated. In other cases, the techniques are traditional but the forms are not. While the possibilities for this kind of eclectic practice are seemingly endless, in successful work the combinations are never arbitrary. This is, in fact, one of the key points about ceramic sculpture of the last three decades. The sculptor may be free to make reference to any previous forms and to employ virtually any techniques— whether or not these are specifically part of the ceramics tradition—but logic must always prevail between these choices. There must be reasons for the selections and combinations characterizing one's work.

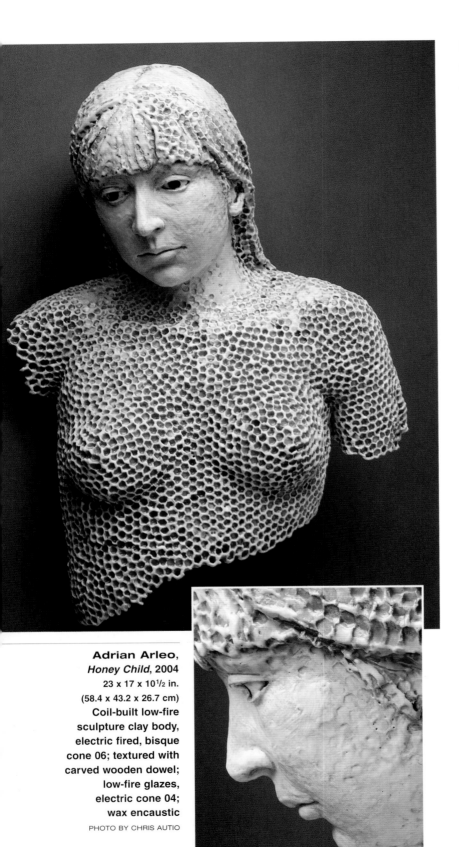

Adrian Arleo,
Honey Child, 2004
23 x 17 x 10½ in.
(58.4 x 43.2 x 26.7 cm)
Coil-built low-fire
sculpture clay body,
electric fired, bisque
cone 06; textured with
carved wooden dowel;
low-fire glazes,
electric cone 04;
wax encaustic
PHOTO BY CHRIS AUTIO

In successful sculpture the marriage of technique and style is closely connected to content. Sculptors can, and often do, use this connection strategically. As Mark Burns has observed, attractive works that reflect a mastery of traditional techniques tend to be more readily accepted by the ceramics community than those that appear experimental or, worse yet, poorly crafted. On the one hand, if one deals with controversial content, a skillful employment of traditional techniques may make the work less vulnerable to knee-jerk rejection. On the other hand, a representation of conventional subject matter, such as a human head, may acquire provocative content through the use of unorthodox techniques or the combination of conflicting stylistic influences. Knowing this, the sculptor considers content and makes choices about technique and style while gauging a work's potential effect on an audience.

Ideally, the meaning of a work depends as much on the method of construction and the particular style of its forms as on any narrative that it may convey through representation. For example, the apparently simple decision to model rather than to carve, mold, or assemble a sculpture can significantly affect meanings conveyed by the final form. Selection of techniques that involve manipulating clay into hollow forms as opposed to working it in solid masses is even more consequential. Because the vessel has been so prominent within the ceramics tradition, voids in clay tend to suggest containment rather than mere emptiness. One can exploit this connection—as Adrian Arleo does when she draws analogies between her hollow, coil-built figures and bird nests, hollow stumps, or cages of bare branches—or one can resist it. Arthur González, although employing a pinch-pot technique to produce his hollow nudes, treats clay not as the boundary of a vessel but rather as a skin pressed outward as if by bone and muscle or, more poetically, by emotions welling up from a hidden and therefore mysterious inner source.

Doug Jeck's manner of creating hollow forms from slabs pressed simultaneously from within and from without contributes directly to the impression of a vein-popping dynamic of energies in his weirdly immobile figures. The meeting of internal and external forces in a thin clay wall serves for Jeck as a metaphor for the conflict of private, psychological pressures and the outer demands of public life. Christyl Boger, who builds with coils then, like Jeck, adjusts her forms by pushing outward while compressing from the exterior, describes this conflict of forces in terms of a tension between the "animal" and the "cultured" body. Another kind of contrast is sought by Justin Novak, whose method of pinching up his hollow figures bit by bit from the base requires that decisions be made about parts—legs, torso, arms—while the whole remains merely an idea. The earthy humanity that results from this technique is deliberately at odds with Novak's formal references to the idealized ceramic sculpture of 18th-century European salons.

Although the material properties of clay and its physical transformations during firing encourage the ceramic sculptor to work in hollow format, some prefer the heft of solid forms. Michaelene Walsh's sculptures, for example, seem hewn from heavy blocks rather than

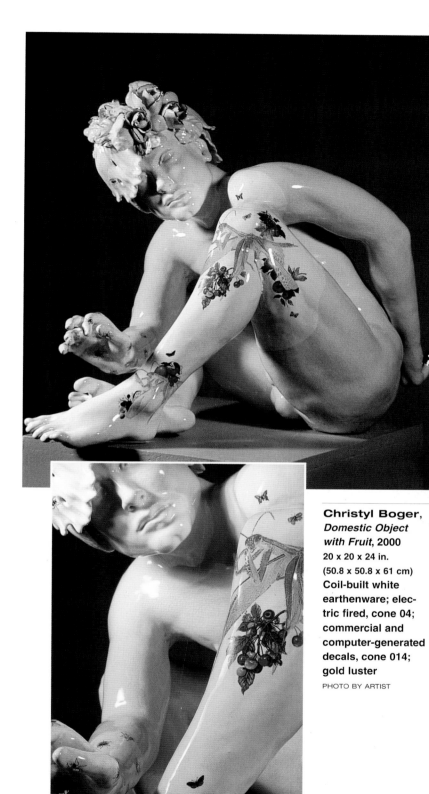

Christyl Boger,
Domestic Object with Fruit, **2000**
20 x 20 x 24 in.
(50.8 x 50.8 x 61 cm)
Coil-built white earthenware; electric fired, cone 04; commercial and computer-generated decals, cone 014; gold luster
PHOTO BY ARTIST

Michaelene Walsh,
Monkey Head Cup,
2003
5½ x 4 x 4 in.
(14 x 10.2 x 10.2 cm)
**Slab-built red
earthenware;
electric fired,
cone 05; glazes**

Arthur González,
*The Legacy of Cara
Triste*, 2000
34 x 24 x 11 in.
(86.4 x 61 x 27.9 cm)
**Coil-built low-fire
red clay; gas fired in
reduction, cone 2;
blown glass,
gold leaf, epoxy,
engobes, whiskey**

developed out of a process metaphorical of organic growth. As a consequence, her gnomish, articulated doll or puppetlike figures strike an uneasy balance between the animate and the inanimate. Working her dense forms with a minimum of tools, she achieves rough, primal surfaces. The unsettling effects of her works—which comment on the subconscious projection of ideas and emotions onto objects—are achieved through the disparity between the familiarity and innocence of toys and the uncanny irregularity of her surfaces.

The evidence of hand-building processes can produce expressive effects in ceramic sculpture, but its absence can be equally meaningful. Molding techniques are the most common for achieving an impression of detachment from the human hand. This impression can be used for very different purposes. Mark Burns's sleek forms are, for example, intentionally evocative of the popular decorative arts of the 1950s, when brightly colored monochrome panther lamps prowled the tops of televisions in American living rooms. Molding thus serves to connect Burns's works to mass-produced objects that are very much of this world. In contrast, Nan Smith's technique of molding is employed specifically to create an otherworldly effect: the impression of the figure's transcendence of materiality and existence in a realm of pure consciousness. Ironically, molding from a living model serves in Smith's sculptures as a means of stressing the absence of the physical body.

The effects of technique can be difficult to separate from the quality in sculpture that we generally describe as style, since both influence the particular appearance of forms. Style can, in fact, sometimes seem merely a consequence of certain techniques, as, for example, in some pre-Columbian figures in which a rigid, schematic appearance results from slab construction. In contemporary ceramic sculpture, however, style is rarely incidental. It tends to be chosen as consciously as technique. In many cases, style is invoked as a reference to particular periods in the past, as is the case in Justin Novak's rococo-inspired figurines or Mark Burns's revival of 1950s design. In Akio Takamori's recent work, stylistic references are triply significant, pointing simultaneously to fashion in 17th-century Spain, the personal style of the baroque painter Diego Velázquez, and the style of applying paint to canvas as opposed to glazing ceramic surfaces.

It is clear that in matters of both style and technique, choice has become the key concept in today's ceramic sculpture. What the sculptors in this book have in common, apart from their obvious focus on the figure, is a drive to explore new ways of realizing this timeless subject matter through the selection and combination of techniques and elements of style. This selection and combination draw on a seemingly infinite resource of possibilities in the past and present, but they are always carried out in concert with the determination of content. The result is a tremendous sense of visual variety in contemporary ceramic sculpture and at the same time a strong feeling of propriety and coherence, of the participation of today's sculptors in a process of giving meaning and value to diversity. Of all the ways in which sculpture can be conceived, perhaps none could be more appropriate than this as a reflection of our times.

GLEN R. BROWN, PH.D.
ASSOCIATE PROFESSOR OF ART HISTORY
KANSAS STATE UNIVERSITY

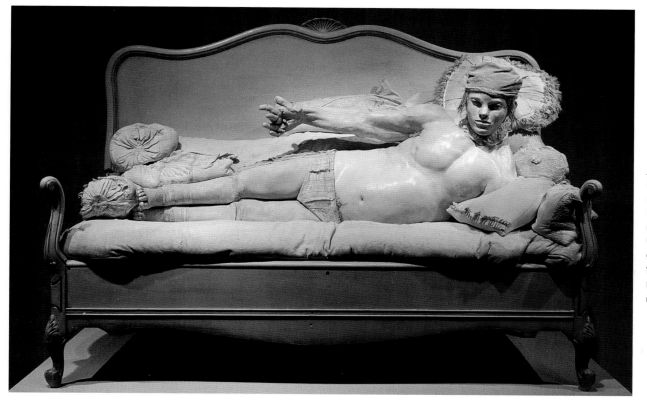

Doug Jeck, *Study in Antique White*, 2002
54 x 60 x 40 in.
(1.4 x 1.5 x 1 m)
Coil-built porcelain; electric fired, cone 4; fabric, wood, hair, mixed media
PHOTO BY KATE PREFTAKES

Adrian Arleo
BODY LANGUAGE

AS A CHILD, I ALWAYS ENJOYED "ARTS AND CRAFTS" AS A FORM

of playing. I discovered early on, though, that when an object conveyed emotion, it became powerful beyond mere play. This power is what became, and continues to be, my motivation in making art. I have a black-and-white print of myself at age six, caught in the act of discovering this power. The photo was taken by my mother at the Metropolitan Museum of Art in New York City. I'm standing in front of Andrew Wyeth's painting *Christina's World*, and the way I'm staring up at the stranded, reclining woman in the painting reminds me of the intense wonder and recognition I'd experienced. Somehow, through the gesture Wyeth had given her, I knew exactly what Christina was feeling.

Adrian Arleo,
***Honey Child I** (detail), 2004*
23 x 17 x 10½ in.
(58.4 x 43.2 x 26.7 cm)
**Coil-built low-fire sculpture
clay body, electric fired,
bisque cone 06; textured
with carved wooden dowel;
low-fire glazes, electric
cone 04; wax encaustic**
PHOTO BY CHRIS AUTIO

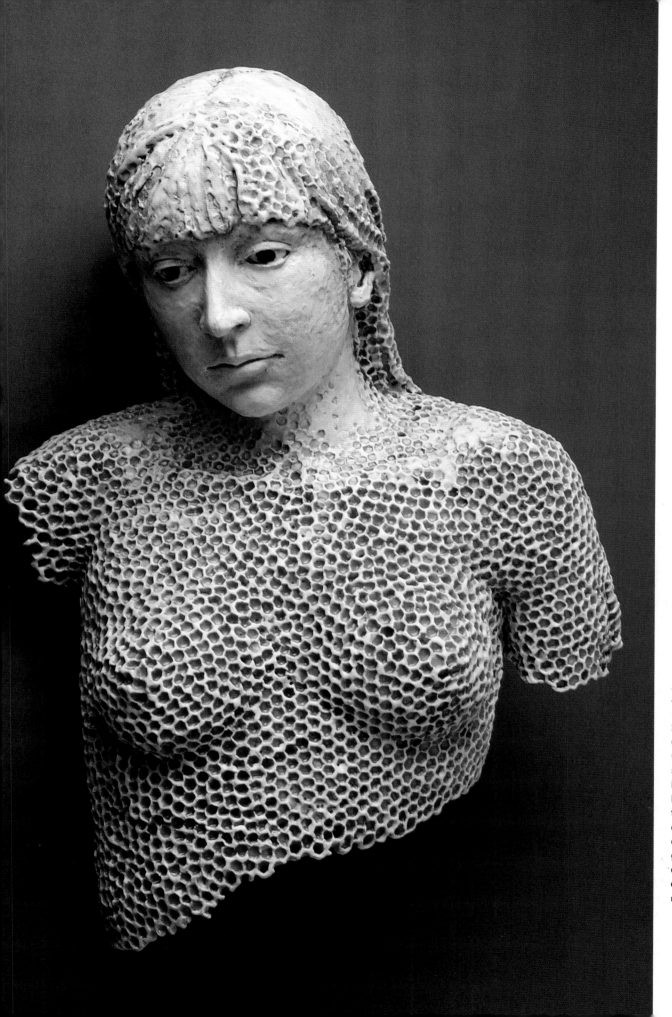

Adrian Arleo,
Honey Child I, 2004
23 x 17 x 10$\frac{1}{2}$ in.
(58.4 x 43.2 x 26.7 cm)
Coil-built low-fire
sculpture clay
body, electric fired,
bisque cone 06;
textured with
carved wooden
dowel; low-fire
glazes, electric
cone 04; wax
encaustic

PHOTO BY CHRIS AUTIO

Some artists must traverse a long and circuitous road to find their medium. I was lucky to discover clay at an early age. My engagement began somewhat ignominiously, with the classic lumpy, pinched animal projects in grade school. When I was about 10, my older brother started taking pottery classes. Intrigued by the garbage can full of reject clay and slurry, I tried my hand at a horse head that ended up having the appearance of an animal emerging from a stormy sea; its neck was arched, its mane seemed windswept, and its gesture contained some sort of drama that made my heart pound. That was it for me: I was sold on clay.

In 1979 I entered Pitzer College in Claremont, California, where I studied art and anthropology. Because the art department was small, and run by the ceramic artist David Furman, it focused mainly on clay. I became interested in slab-built, low-fire sculpture. I avoided the potter's wheel, glaze chemistry, and the gas kiln. I liked the control I could get with an electric kiln; I didn't like to leave anything to chance. My work consisted of surreal boxed landscapes, some with fish swimming into or out of the box, others with cacti growing on the box, which later evolved into a small series of cactuslike human figures. All were impeccably crafted, with clean edges and accurate, realistic underglaze finishes.

Of all the features of the body, it's the face that most intrigues and challenges me.

Upon entering the MFA program at Rhode Island School of Design in 1984, I received a rude but helpful awakening. During my first grad-school critique with then-head Jacquelyn Rice, I was devastated by her assessment that my work was coming from the school of "tight is right." Jacquie was so sure I needed to loosen up that she vetoed my use of slabs, then gave me a new assignment: work only with coils. Her assumption was that this method would cause me to work more loosely, with fewer preconceptions. Twenty years later I continue to have pretty strong preconceptions about most of my sculptures, but I'm still working only with coils. And my interest in the human form began in earnest with this change in building methods.

The idea that my work was "tight" struck me as some kind of sin and jolted me toward a new kind of imagery. Movement, sensuality, and a subtle suggestion of the figure became the first antidote to that tightness. I began moving toward the human figure by coiling twisted, tubular forms that more closely resembled sea slugs than humans. For me, building with slabs had felt almost like woodworking in that it consisted of cutting slabs to certain specific shapes and dimensions, then joining them. With coils, I would start building at one end, with a comparatively modest conception of where the piece was heading, and figure out the form as I went.

At this time I also began to experiment with terra sigillata as an alternative to underglazes. To visually activate the smooth surface of the clay, I layered different colors of terra sigillata, then sanded down through the layers with superfine steel wool to reveal colors and create patterns. After lightly dampening the surface in small sections at a time, I'd buff the sig to a sheen with a piece of plastic bag. I found butterfly wings and shells endless sources of inspiration for different pallets of color and pattern variations.

To become more informed about the human body, I began to study what we could call "figure sculpture's greatest hits": the Cycladic figures, Roman and Greek statues, and the work of Leonardo da Vinci, Michelangelo, Auguste Rodin, Alberto Giacometti, Manuel Neri, Stephen DeStaebler (where are the women?), and Louise Bourgeois. I also learned, from the cast plaster figures of Pompeii, how the most unplanned, defensive, or helpless gestures can convey devastating emotional impact through the mysterious power of body language.

Adrian Arleo,
Nest Arms, 2004
30 x 27 x 27 in.
(76.2 x 68.6 x 68.6 cm)
Coil-built low-fire
sculpture clay
body; electric fired,
bisque cone 06;
low-fire glazes,
electric fired,
cone 04; wax
encaustic, wire
PHOTO BY CHRIS AUTIO

Adrian Arleo,
Embodiment, 2004
23 x 17 x 10½ in.
(58.4 x 43.2 x 26.7 cm)
Coil-built low-fire
sculpture clay
body, electric fired,
bisque cone 06;
press-molded
hands; low-fire
glazes, electric
fired, cone 04;
cherry wood,
steel rod

PHOTOS BY CHRIS AUTIO

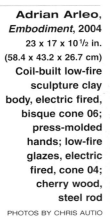

For several semesters my grad school imagery went through some awkward transitions. The sea slugs grew more "humanesque" but held on stubbornly to forms and coloration that referred to an undersea environment. Not till I allowed the human form to emerge undisguised did the content begin to come clear, and narratives begin to unfold.

Solving Sculpting Problems

When I worked with the human figure, issues of scale immediately came into play. To deal with life-size forms and the limitations of my kiln size, I learned about sectioning pieces by cutting them apart in such a way as to make the line as inconspicuous as possible. Some artists—Viola Frey, for example—use blocklike sections as a part of the composition and content of the work. I prefer to hide the sections within the form and texture. With standing figures it's easiest to make the division at the waist, or under the buttocks around to the groin. With a seated figure, cutting off the head around the jaw and along the hairline is usually a good way to camouflage the line. To avoid distortion of the form when it's taken apart, the clay should be quite stiff before sectioning it. Laying the sections on thick foam rubber helps keep the shape intact while a large flange, or lip (its size depends on the size of the piece), is built into the inside of the top piece. The flange needs to fit securely into the lower section.

Another useful tool for building and displaying tall, narrow, stacked, or tippy pieces is a steel base and threaded steel rod. I like to use a simple design in which the rod is removable for shipping. A short piece of threaded steel rod is welded to the center of a steel plate, and a suitably sized connector nut is used to attach any length of threaded steel rod to the short piece that was welded on. Most often the rod needs to go only about halfway up inside the piece. When building a piece on a rod, cover it with a thin layer of newspaper so that if the clay shrinks, the piece won't get stuck. Internal clay "spokes" are used to hold the sculpture in place on the rod.

In building large pieces I've found that by using fairly stiff clay and a consistent wall thickness (¾ to 1 inch [1.9 to 2.5 cm]), and by carefully pacing the drying of the figure, I can solve slumping and cracking problems. This in turn allows the forms to be more structurally complex. And, as shown in the next section, using coils lengthwise for legs and arms is a more efficient way to create narrow forms. Lengthwise coils also aid in the angling and positioning process. (Adding coils round and round, horizontally, can lead to sagging and cracking.) Making small, internal, crescent-shaped clay support buttresses also helps stabilize the forms.

Sources and Inspiration

I usually begin a piece with pencil sketches of ideas, then refine the image and work out three-dimensional issues through maquettes. As far as anatomy goes, I'm of the same mind as Nathan Goldstein, who, in his book *Figure Drawing*, writes, "We should recognize that the artist, unlike the anthropologist, does better to support his perceptions with intuition than with calipers." I'm concerned with making the figure accurate enough that nothing is proportionally distracting, but not so obsessively rendered that "life-likeness" or "accuracy" becomes the main focus. I consistently prefer to make heads proportionally on the small side, because I find large heads awkward looking. I probably make legs a little too long, hands sometimes small, sometimes big, depending on the content of the particular piece. I seem to start with feet too small. Almost all of my pieces have a tendency to grow as I work.

Of all the features of the body, it's the face that most intrigues and challenges me. During the 20 years I've worked with the figure, the faces have moved steadily from vagueness toward increasing specificity and recognizability. The eyes, when I was starting out, were undefined; they have since evolved from being closed, to being downward turned, to being open and forthrightly gazing.

I almost always play with how specific to get with facial features. I prefer facial expressions to be quiet,

Adrian Arleo, *Wasp Nest—Three Figures*, 2004. 16 x 13 x 8 in. (40.6 x 33 x 20.3 cm). Coil-built low-fire sculpture clay body, electric fired, bisque cone 06; textured with carved wooden dowel; low-fire glazes, electric fired, cone 04; cherry wood, steel rod.
PHOTO BY CHRIS AUTIO

introverted, or even somewhat blank, suggesting that the person is experiencing an internal moment rather than trying to actively confront the viewer. In my most recent body of work I've swung back and forth between very specific faces (including a portrait of my daughter in *Honey Child I*) to no features at all (as in *Wasp Nest—Three Figures*, or the standing figure *Embodiment*).

The Psyche As Form

In recent pieces I've been thinking about the concepts of *recognition* and *identification*. Something in us naturally responds to a *specific* visage. In recognizing a face that is "familiar," empathy is a frequent response. Yet there is a reversal at play here too. Sometimes a work of art taps more deeply into us when it has no specific features, and so resonates as an archetype.

My main conceptual concern in working with the figure doesn't stem from a fascination with the construction and problem-solving process. Nor is it just the beauty of the human form that holds me. What continues to absorb me is how, by rendering the physical body, one can convey, or at least suggest, a remarkable array of nonphysical, internal, ephemeral, spiritual, emotional, or psychological experiences. I use the human form to get at the human being and human nature, not at the body as an end in itself.

I find the nesting and nurturing instincts of wild creatures to be a powerful creative role model.

For years I've worked with themes of metamorphosis. Arms, legs, or heads are transforming into other creatures, perhaps as we ourselves are transformed in our fantasies, intuitions, and dreams. In most of these pieces I feel that the animal, bird, or other creature has been hidden within the human and is emerging in a way that suggests the person's internal state or character. In some cases the revealed state is benign; in others it's ambiguous; in still others it's deeply disturbing.

Tangential to the metamorphosis theme are references to textures and shapes found in nature. In order to avoid a trivial fascination with "nakedness" and tap into more poetic renderings of the human body, I've refrained from creating fleshlike surfaces and have instead developed a wide range of textures that suggest organic and inorganic substances. Deep scorations in the clay can suggest wood or water; porous, open surfaces can allude to rock, coral, or beehives. Many of these textures are created by pushing into the clay with simple wooden tools. Some tools are carved to create specific effects, as with my wasp's nest comb. For this texture, I whittled the end of a wooden dowel into a hexagon, then carefully aligned and pressed 1/4-inch-deep (6 mm) holes into almost leather-hard clay. Glazes can give added depth when used as washes and/or layers. I gravitate toward dry, opaque glazes that don't show brush strokes; the glazes listed at the end of this chapter are old favorites that work well together. The Sand Dry base glaze is excellent as a wash in textured areas. I wipe the surface clean of glaze and apply a coat or two of the Stony Lithium base glaze over it. The Sand Dry saturates through and gives wonderful depth to the texture.

After the final firing of *Gathering*, wax encaustic was melted in a double boiler and quickly painted on some areas of the piece while the wax was still flowing on the brush. A heat gun was used to further melt and adhere it to the surface. The wax has a thick satin quality that complements the dry surface of the Stony Lithium base glaze and gives it a more finished look, with areas highlighted with its sheen. The birds were first fired with terra sigillata as a dense base coat. Casein was painted over the fired sig to enhance the color and add a layer of translucency that mimics the shimmer of feathers.

In recent years I've focused on nests of different kinds. This interest stems from a desire to find refuge and solace through intimate observation, stillness, and empathy with, and in, the other-than-

**Adrian Arleo,
Plumage, 2004**
21 x 15½ x 15 in.
(53.3 x 39.4 x 38.1 cm)
**Coil-built low-fire
sculpture clay
body, electric fired,
bisque cone 06;
press-molded
hands; low-fire
glazes, electric
fired, cone 04**
PHOTO BY CHRIS AUTIO

human world. Again, a certain evolution has been at play. I was first drawn to nest imagery in 1989, when I was considering becoming pregnant. When this procreative energy welled up, I suddenly saw my own body as an abode—a place of nurture for another—and a group of human/nest sculptures was my response. The nest imagery I've been drawn to more recently, in contrast, comes less from my own experience and more from observing the procreative drive in the natural world. I find the nesting and nurturing instincts of wild creatures to be a powerful creative role model. It also reassures me that creation knows exactly what it's doing, even when human beings seem not to.

TECHNIQUE: COIL

Adrian Arleo,
Gathering
(detail), 2004
PHOTO BY
CHRIS AUTIO

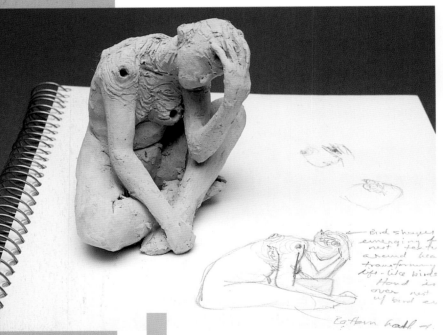

2 The artist's source material

3 One-inch-diameter (2.5 cm) coils are extruded then rolled to compress the stretched clay. I usually extrude about 25 pounds (11.4 kg) of clay at a time and allow the coils to lay out on the work surface to stiffen up to the right firmness. For me, that means the clay will be firm enough that I can quickly build a large form without any sagging. The coils are then wrapped in plastic and occasionally sprayed with water to maintain the right level of moisture.

1 A rough sketch and a small model of the piece are made to refine the idea and work out three-dimensional problems.

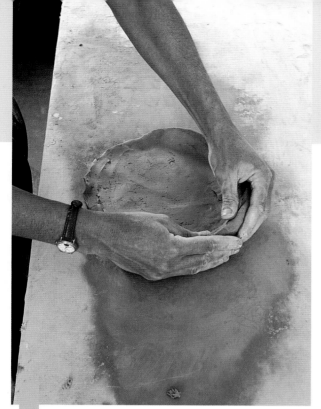

4 To start a seated figure, the bottom of the piece is made from a pounded-out slab about 3/4 inch (1.9 cm) thick.

6 This figure is going to have one leg resting as in a cross-legged position, and the other leg will have the knee drawn up. To begin the leg that's lower, the underside of the thigh is first created with coils extended out lengthwise, with a support block and foam rubber under them.

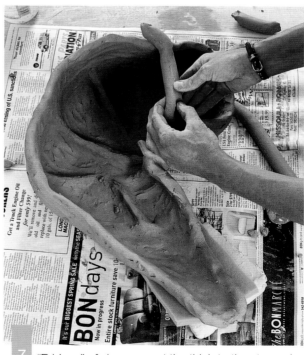

5 I put the slab on several sheets of newspaper so that when the piece dries, it won't stick to the work surface. The edges of the clay are curled up and reinforced with coils—like buttresses—to help support the area; later, when the piece gets larger, there'll be a lot of weight and stress here. Other areas of stress, such as where the *glutaeus maximus* meet, need to be reinforced as well to avoid splitting apart.

7 "Bridges" of clay connect the thigh to the stomach.

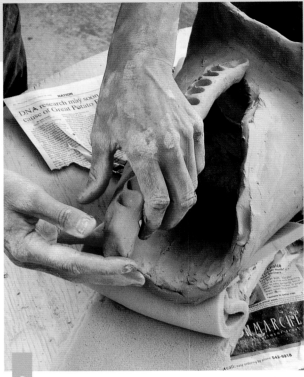

8   When using the coils lengthwise, I work back and forth from one side to the other, coming up the sides and meeting in a V shape. Later, smaller coils will be added that come around and form the knee.

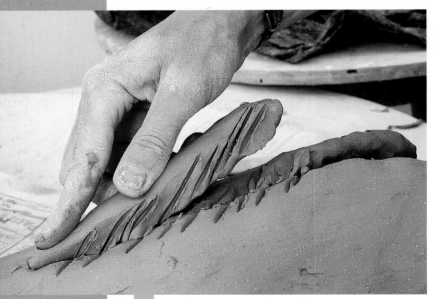

9   The V is filled in by pressing the two sides together and filling it with a coil. Scoring is a good idea in these places.

10   At this point, I'm working on three cylindrical forms, rotating from one to another to keep the weight balanced. A thick "spine" is added to create a more rigid back; it will help support the curve of the form later.

11   A hole or two needs to be cut out of the bottom of the form to help relieve stress and aid in drying. Without holes, large cracks can occur across the flat surface during drying and firing. When a hole is cut out, it's important to compress its edge with my finger to ensure that cracks don't develop. I make sure not to compress the edges by pushing down, making them thin and papery. Instead, I push in to thicken them.

12 The form can be altered at any point. Here, the buttocks are enlarged by first making a low horizontal cut, then, from the inside, the form is pushed out, scored, and filled with a coil. A rubber rib and paddle are used to sculpt the surface.

14 Building up the back of the torso, keeping the weight balanced with the legs. It's very important that I pay attention to the balance of the form. If too much leg is built before there's enough weight in the torso, the form can tip and rock forward, distorting the bottom of the piece and messing up the proportions. This is particularly critical when building a figure with both legs drawn up. It's a good idea to keep the edges that aren't being worked on wrapped in plastic.

13 Paddling the thigh. While working out the leg with the knee drawn up, the thigh was coiled at an angle to help keep the curve of the form. The back of the knee area was left out because the calf will be against it.

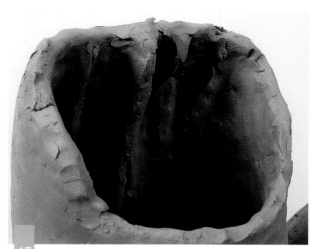

15 Supports inside the back

16 To create the lower part of the leg, I add coils lengthwise from the back of the knee area down to the work surface, extending several out to form the bottom of the foot. Add more lengthwise coils to form the calf muscle; continue around to meet approximately at the shin.

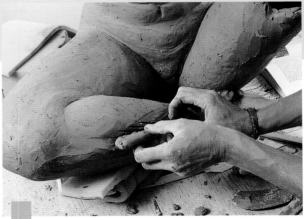

18 To close off the form, I score the two sides and add a scored coil, then use my hands or a tool to smooth the area. At this point there's enough weight in the legs to cause stress on some joints; I check to make sure there's no cracking or separation where the thighs meet the stomach or hip. If I see cracks, I score the area, add a coil, and compress the surface. I check the interior for cracking too. Sometimes, due to the weight of the wet clay, cracks can start inside the bottom of the figure. If they do, I compress, score, and add a coil.

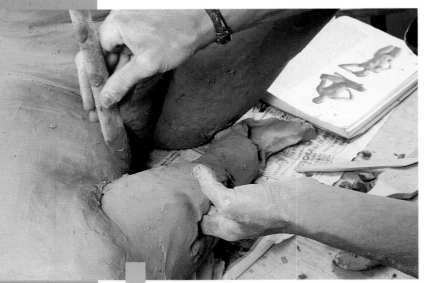

17 Modeling the calf by pushing the clay in and out. I add more clay to any areas that get thin.

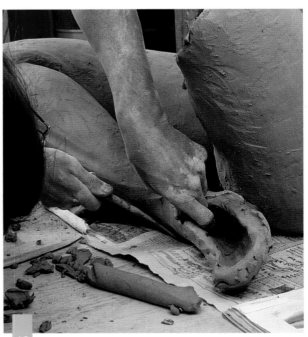

19 The foot is formed from the lengthwise coils extending out from the bottom of the leg. These coils make up the bottom of the foot. More coils are added to make the sides...

20 ...then smaller ones are added to bridge over and fill down to the toes. In this way, a general foot "wedge" is formed. Later, the definition of toes and bones will be modeled and carved.

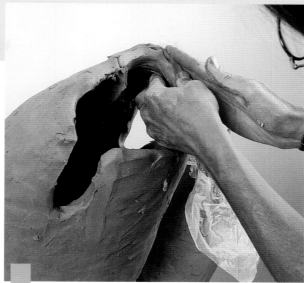

22 The shoulders are covered from front to back. Note the spine support up the back; later it will continue up into the neck as well. The shoulders are reinforced with buttresses too. With the shoulders covered, more definition can be given to the torso. Breasts will come later.

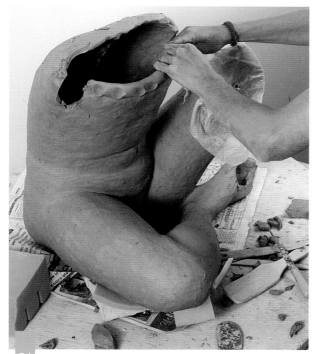

21 When the back is getting tall, I cut a V out of each armpit area to start to define the broadness of the back and shoulders.

23 The lower half of the second leg is started, as with the other, using lengthwise coils.

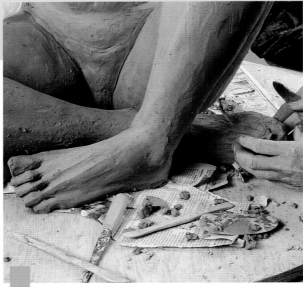

24 More coils are added around and down into the foot. At this point the detail on the feet is carved and modeled with wooden tools.

26 Scoring the edges (the clay of the torso may be a bit drier than the new clay) and adding coils to form the breast.

25 While the armholes are still open, the breasts are made by cutting two open U shapes into the chest. I position where they'll be by drawing the lines first, then cutting and roughing out one breast at a time so as not to weaken the chest structure. I push the flap out from the inside and start to give it some shape from the outside.

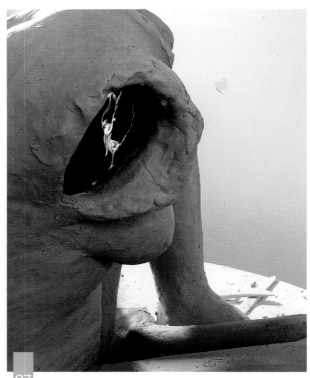

27 After the breasts are done, a structural grid is coiled on the inside of the chest (two horizontal and two vertical coils, one or two coils tall) to add rigidity to the wall so that when the head is added, the chest won't sink in and collapse. This is particularly important when the head leans forward or looks down.

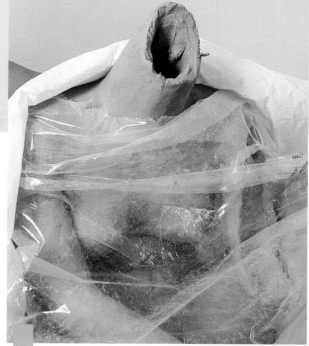

28 Like the legs, the arms are made with lengthwise coils, which is helpful not only for composing the position and proportion of the arm but also aids in making the form more streamlined and easy to adjust. When the undersides and sides are done, the arm and hand will be closed the same way as were the leg and foot.

30 The neck is elongated so that it will fit inside the head. It must be left uncovered to stiffen up while the face is being worked out; otherwise, it will sag with the weight of the head. Since facial features usually take some time, the body is wrapped in plastic to keep it from drying out.

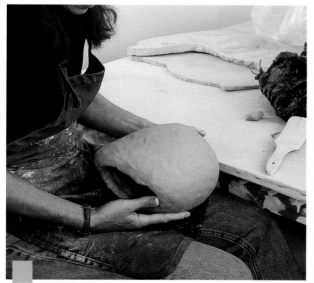

29 The head is made separately by starting with a pinched bowl form making up a "skull cap" the same thickness as the rest of the figure; coils are then added, and a general head/skull shape is formed. The benefit of making the head separately is that it can be held up to the body and easily altered to the right proportion before it's attached. I find this to be much easier than building the head, from the chin up, directly on the piece.

31 Features such as eye sockets are pushed in, and the cheeks and chin are pushed out. The nose and lips are made from small coils added to the scored surface, then defined with tools. I find eyes to be the toughest feature to get right. I often wait to finish them until after the head is attached to the body and I can orient them to fit the overall gesture and feeling of the piece. I used a photo as a reference for the face because I really liked the simplicity and tranquility of the features.

32 Attaching the head. The inside of the jaw is heavily scored, then inserted over the elongated neck, which has been scored on the outside. The top of the head is then cut off, and the interior neck is pressed against the inside of the head for reinforcing the connection. Coils are then added around the jaw to create a smooth transition and add strength.

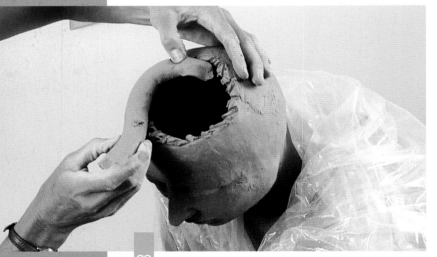

33 The top of the skull can be scored and reattached if the head seems to be the right size and shape. Often, however, I need to alter the shape. This can be done in a variety of ways. Here, a V shape is cut out to make the head smaller; small coils are added to the scored, pressed-together edges, and the overall form is paddled and sculpted with tools. Finally, the hole is coiled in and paddled a little more. When paddling, support the head so that you don't weaken the neck or alter its position.

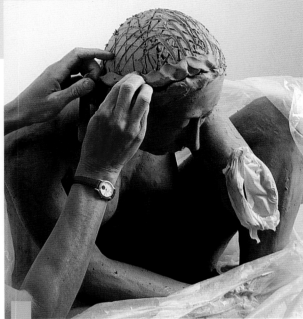

34 Hair is created by scoring the scalp and adding smaller coils. If the hair will be very thick in some areas, it's a good idea to use a thin tool to poke holes through the thick spots to aerate the clay and allow moisture to escape more easily when drying and firing. This aerating technique can be used anywhere on the piece wherever I think the clay may have gotten a little too thick (with most sculpture bodies, more than 1 inch [2.5 cm]). The holes' outsides can be smoothed over.

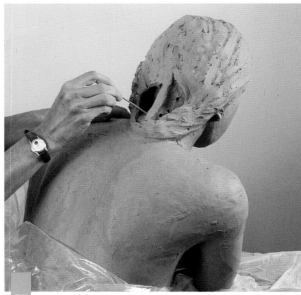

35 If an air pocket is created between the neck and the hair, I poke holes through to the inside of the piece.

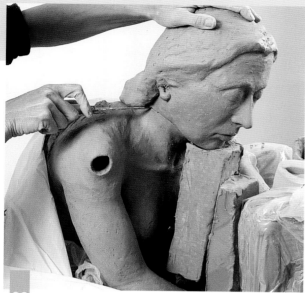

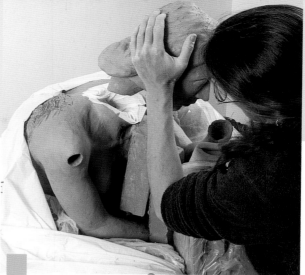

36 To fit the piece in the kiln, I cut off the head at the jaw line, first incising the line before cutting it with a clean fettling knife. I prefer to cut straight in rather than at an angle. Due to the angle of this head, supports had to be used to keep the head from falling forward. These blocks will need to stay in place for the drying process to ensure that the head doesn't tip and distort the neck. The head will be epoxied in place after all firings are done.

38 Adding toilet paper to the rim so the clay won't stick together, then putting the head back on. I use a rib or wooden tool to clean up the connection, which may entail taking the head off a few times to shave off clay from the flange for a proper fit. I gently lift the head up and down to make sure it's easy to remove then clean its edges of any thin overhangs or crumbs that would later break off and look sloppy. I dry the piece with the head on, checking it every now and then to make sure it doesn't shrink so much that it sticks. After the piece is glazed and finished, the head can be epoxied on permanently or left removable so that the sculpture may be shipped in a smaller crate.

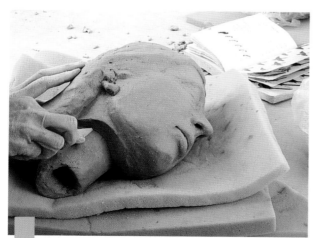

37 Cleaning up the edges and trimming the inside of the neck so there'll be room for a lip, or flange. I score the inside edge of the rim of the head and add coils to create a flange that's long enough to secure the head in place.

39 The second hand on this piece is made separately by attaching a clump of coils together, then carving the fingers with a wooden tool.

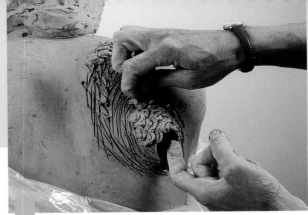

40 The hand is attached by tapering and scoring the wrist so it will fit inside the scored, open end of the arm. Coils are then added to secure the joint and create a smooth transition.

42 This piece is textured with little globs of clay meant to imitate the surface of cliff swallow mud nests. A slurry is made up of dry, crushed clay mixed with vinegar and Patch-A-Tatch, a ceramic mender made by Duncan. Little balls of clay are dipped into the slurry, then pressed onto the scored surface. The slurry helps to create a more natural, irregular-looking surface.

43 Birds are pinched and carved from solid clay, then hollowed by sticking a thin wooden tool down the length of the body to aid in drying and firing. Holes are made for the legs and feet, which will be created out of wire (not to be fired) and painted and epoxied to the piece after the last firing.

41 Since the head had to be sectioned to fit in the kiln, the hand is also too high and must be removed. The least noticeable place to make this section is at the elbow. The arm will be epoxied back on after the final firing. The inside of the cut is textured with incised lines to give the epoxy something to grab onto.

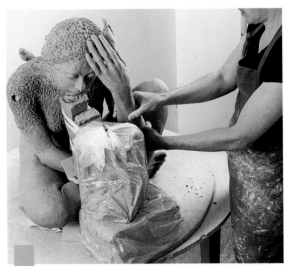

44 The piece is now ready to dry. The arm will dry on a piece of foam rubber, and the head will stay in place, on the supports.

Adrian Arleo,
Gathering, 2004
25 x 23 x 22 in.
(63.5 x 58.4 x 55.9 cm)
Coil-built stoneware;
electric cone 06; glaze
cone 04; wax encaustic
on figure; terra sigillata,
casein paint, and
wire on birds
PHOTO BY CHRIS AUTIO

STONY LITHIUM BASE GLAZE

This glaze is very dry and works well alone (as a white base), with colorants, or layered with other glazes. Try the glaze over a dark, glossy one that has been applied in a textured area. Fire to cone 06–05.

Lithium carbonate	15.6
EPK	22
Flint	45
Bentonite	3.7
Ferro Frit 3110	13.7
Total	**100**

Colorants

Gray

Mason Stain 6500 Sage Gray	2

Brown

Iron chromate	5

LOW-FIRE WHITE SCULPTURE CLAY BODY

Fire to cone 06–04. Due to the large amount of fire clay in it, this clay body can be fired to higher temperatures. It has been known to do well in anagama firings reaching cone 10 to 11. However, it's always smart to do a test first.

Greenstripe or AP Green fire clay	36
OM4 ball clay	27
EPK	9
Talc	10
Wollastonite	9
Flint	9
Total	**100**

Add

Fine grog	10
Medium grog	15
Nylon fiber	30–40 grams

SAND DRY BASE GLAZE

This glaze is good for using as a wash in texture; it's compatible with Stony Lithium Base Glaze, below. Fire to cone 06–04.

Gerstley borate (or substitute)	50
Nepheline syenite	17
Alumina hydrate	33
Total	**100**

Colorants

Lighter Blue-Gray

Copper carbonate	3.75
Cobalt carbonate	0.85

Very Dark Blue-Black

Copper carbonate	3.75
Cobalt carbonate	3.75
Iron chromate	1.85

Chestnut Brown

Red iron oxide	18
Manganese dioxide	8

Lighter Brown

Iron chromate	13.5

Dark Green

Copper carbonate	18
Iron chromate	8

Nylon fiber in the clay body

GALLERY
OF INVITED ARTISTS

Debra W. Fritts, *Lady with Bird Dress*, 2003
33 x 14 x 11 in. (83.8 x 35.6 x 27.9 cm)
Coil-built terra cotta; electric fired, bisque cone 2;
multi-fired slips, glazes, underglazes, oxides,
cone 04; red thread
PHOTO BY MIKE JENSON

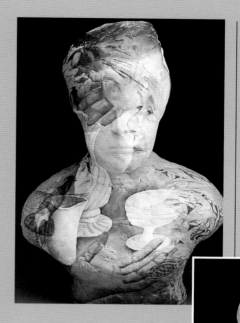

Kate Blacklock,
Still Lives, 2002
23 x 17 x 10 in.
(58.4 x 43.2 x 25.4 cm)
Slab- and press-molded
porcelain; electric fired,
cone 6; oil-painted
surface
PHOTOS BY ARTIST

**Ronna
Neuenschwander**,
Dji Tala (Water Carrier),
2003
35 x 17 x 11 in.
(88.9 x 43.2 x 27.9 cm)
Slip-cast and
assembled earthen-
ware; electric fired,
cone 05; sawdust fired
with terra sigillata;
water pot shard
mosaic, stone
PHOTO BY AARON JOHANSON

Christine Federighi, *Dark Dreamer,* 2004
24 x 6 x 5 in. (61 x 15.2 x 12.7 cm)
Coil-built, assembled, and carved ceramic; cone 04; oil patina
PHOTO BY BONNIE SEEMAN

Christina Lida Bothwell, *Family (Twins),* 2004
Left: 6 x 5 x 4 in. (15.2 x 12.7 x 10.2 cm);
right: 16 x 8 x 5 in. (40.6 x 20.3 x 12.7 cm)
Pit-fired raku clay; electric fired, cone 1;
mold-formed cast glass
PHOTO BY MARLIN WAGNER

Judy Moonelis, *Pair #1,* 2000
10 x 8 x 3 in. (25.4 x 20.3 x 7.6 cm)
Pinched porcelain; electric fired, cone 7; oxides
PHOTO BY MALCOLM VARON

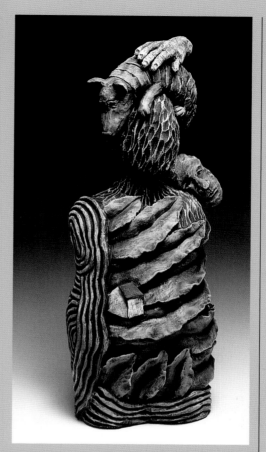

Christine Federighi, *Canine Dreams*, 2004
24 x 6 x 5 in. (61 x 15.2 x 12.7 cm)
Coil-built, assembled, and carved ceramic;
cone 04; oil patina

PHOTO BY ARTIST

Mark D. Chatterley, *Blue Figure*, 2004
72 x 12 x 18 in. (1.8 x .31 x .46 m)
Slab-built stoneware; gas fired, cone 6;
crater glaze

PHOTO BY ARTIST

David Regan,
Snake Tureen, 2000
30 x 13 x 12 in. (76.2 x 33 x 30.5 cm)
Porcelain

PHOTO BY ARTIST

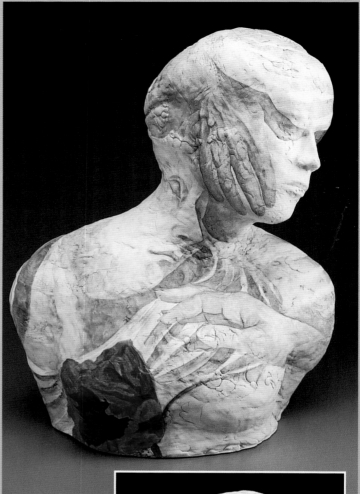

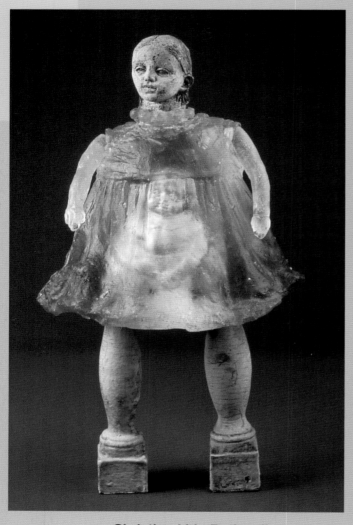

Christina Lida Bothwell,
My Heart Is Like a Butterfly, 2004
20 x 10 x 9 in. (50.8 x 25.4 x 22.9 cm)
Pit-fired raku clay; electric, cone 1;
mold-formed cast glass, wood posts

PHOTO BY MARLIN WAGNER

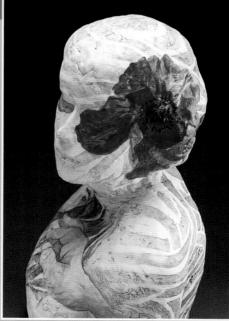

Kate Blacklock, *Poppies*, 2003
21 x 17 x 14 in. (53.3 x 43.2 x 35.6 cm)
Slab-built and press-molded porcelain; electric fired,
cone 6; china paint, cone 018; oils

PHOTOS BY ARTIST

Ronna Neuenschwander, *Ouassala*
(The Satisfied One), 2002
30 x 7 x 7 in. (76.2 x 17.8 x 17.8 cm)
Slip-cast and assembled earthenware; electric
fired, cone 05; sawdust fired with terra sigillata;
water pot shard mosaic, found metal

PHOTO BY AARON JOHANSON

Adrian Arleo

Adrian Arleo studied art and anthropology at
Pitzer College in Claremont, California, and received her BA in 1983. An MFA in ceramics was awarded to Ms. Arleo in 1986 from the Rhode Island School of Design. She has been exhibiting in solo and group exhibitions for more than 20 years, and her work has appeared in numerous ceramics publications, including *500 Teapots* (Lark, 2002) and *Ceramics: A Potter's Handbook* (Wadsworth, 2002). Ms. Arleo's art resides in many private and public collections, including that of the Microsoft Corporation (Seattle) and the Archie Bray Foundation (Helena, Montana), and it is also represented in several sales galleries, including the Ferrin Gallery (Lenox, Massachusetts). She travels extensively as a visiting artist and presents workshops on figurative ceramic art. The artist lives and works in Lolo, Montana.

Christyl Boger
THE NARRATIVE FIGURE

OFTEN OUR SHARED CULTURAL BEHAVIOR SEEMS LIKE THE MOST fragile and vulnerable of veneers. In my ceramic figures, the glazed surface becomes a defensively decorated human skin, a cultural camouflage that is as fragile and brittle as glass. At first glance, these pieces may seem comfortably familiar, even traditional. On closer inspection, they betray a decidedly contemporary angst. Each one acts out a private drama within the wider theater of social expectations. They reflect the combination of three main concerns: the historical associations of ceramic objects, the contemporary possibilities of the medium, and a love of figurative art. The result is work that delights in the human form, borrows strategically from various sculptural and ceramic traditions, and questions the social and cultural ideas that mediate our behavior.

Christyl Boger,
Couplet (Female),
2000
14 x 20 x 10 in.
(35.6 x 50.8 x 25.4 cm)
Coil-built white earthenware; electric fired, cone 6; commercial decals, gold luster, cone 018
PHOTO BY ARTIST

Christyl Boger,
Off Shore, 2004
30 x 22 x 22 in.
(76.2 x 55.9 x 55.9 cm)
**Coil-built white
earthenware;
electric fired,
cone 04; china
paint, white gold
luster, cone 016
and cone 018**

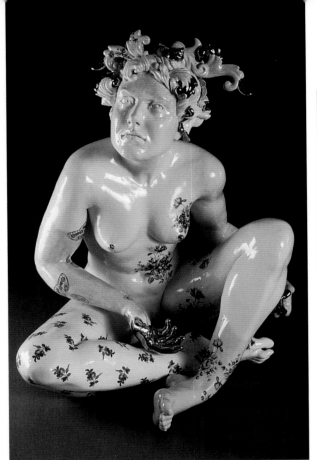

Christyl Boger,
Blue Delft Figure,
2001
26 x 20 x 20 in.
(66 x 50.8 x 50.8 cm)
Coil-built white
earthenware; electric
fired, cone 04;
glazes, cone 04;
commercial decals
cone 015; gold
luster, cone 019
PHOTO BY DOUG HERREN

Story, Scale, and the Figure

There's nothing more exquisitely necessary to each of us than the presence of other people. That makes figuration a powerful visual and psychological hook. The specifics of what is called beautiful may be culturally shaped, but the perception of beauty in the human form seems to be biologically innate. And while we may question the idea of a specific heroic or idealized human form, the language of the body—the emotive quality of gesture and posture—is immanently readable. As social animals, we learn every nuance of this nonverbal language. I see figuration, therefore, as containing an implicit narrative to which I can add my own ideas.

Narrative content is also an element of the traditional ceramic figurine. This sculptural form in miniature is

The very act of making art is political.

loaded with associations of conformity, cliché, decoration, and domesticity. Merging the "story" of a contemporary figure with that of the historical figurine reduces the subject in a way that is more psychological than physical. The size of my work is often smaller than life, but not miniature. The scale invites the viewer to identify with the piece, to see himself or herself represented as this familiar object. The pieces also make reference to the elaborate figurative sculpture of the European baroque and rococo periods. At that time porcelain was as valuable as gold, and income generated by its manufacture was used to finance wars of expansion. In form and function, these objects were inextricably tied to the goals of empire and capital, ideas that founded our contemporary culture.

All of these elements are apparent in the piece I call *Off Shore*. The title can be read as a metaphor for both personal and sociocultural behavior. It alludes to the practice of sheltering money in offshore island-nation banks but also evokes the idea of an imperiled physical or mental state. This is a figure that may be happily paddling about in a vacation paradise, or she might be out to sea in a flimsy life-ring. Its form refers to historical antecedents such as baroque fountain statuary and Degas courtesan ballerinas, in addition to the obvious china figurine. There's humor in the piece, as well as a questioning of one of our most cherished assumptions: that the power and money of our culture can buy not only happiness but also safety and security.

Building

The philosophical and political stance that I take in my art carries over into my studio practice. The very act of making art is political. It implies certain choices about time and how it's used and valued. One of the things that specifically drew me to clay was the "permission to labor" that's implicit in the crafts. I like spending time with the clay; I prefer it to anything else in my working life. I particularly enjoy pinch and coil building, and the way the concentric movements of this type of building echo the spiraling contrapposto rhythms of the finished piece. The pace of the work changes constantly. Sometimes I build quickly, adding or moving a lot of clay at a time. Then there are moments of working very slowly and precisely over the surface. Usually, I'll spend several weeks building each figure.

Our memory of form will never reveal the nuances of direct observation, but working in clay is time consuming, and my poses are generally somewhat uncomfortable and difficult for a model to hold. I solve the problem by thoroughly documenting each pose with a digital camera. The printed images are held in plastic sleeves in a ring binder notebook so that they'll hold up under constant page turning with clay-covered fingers. It's helpful to capture the pose from several vantage points, using high to low angles, and a 360-degree view. I also take detail shots, such as of hands and feet, as well as close-ups of facial expressions. When building, I always use a revolving modeling stand or have a lazy Susan under my ware board. This makes it easy to keep moving the angle from which I work. It also helps reposition the piece in relationship to light sources. Poorly lit or shadowed areas can mask flaws that will show up later.

The starting place for my pieces is always a pinched form, for me the fastest way to move clay into a particular shape. Coil building is an extension of pinching, a way to add more clay and continue extending the wall of the piece. Since I want to add clay quickly, I use coils that are about three times fatter than will be the eventual pinched thickness of the wall. Whenever possible, I add coils without slipping and scoring between them, relying on the compressing action of thorough pinching and ribbing on both the inside and outside to make a strong join. It's important when making coils that they don't become overly dry from excessive rolling or exposure to air. I use a wire tool to cut a wedged block of clay into logs, then make each coil as I need it by quickly squeezing and then briefly rolling it on a damp canvas.

As I build, much of the shape is defined by stretching the wall of the piece from the inside out. The effect is similar to shaping a curved form on a potter's wheel, except with the freedom to move in multiple directions. Similarly, I apply pressure on the outside of the clay wall to move an area in. The edge of a rib can be used to tuck in the creases of folds. When using this kind of directional pressure, remember to support the piece

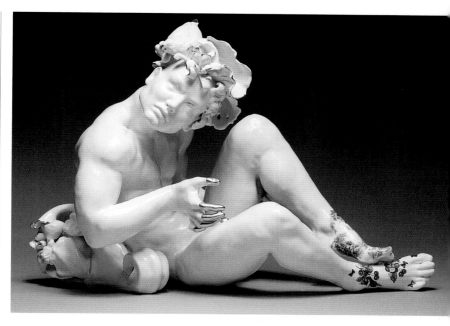

from the opposite side as you move the clay. For example, to create a little fat or muscle bulge, I cup that area on the outside with one hand and use a rib or the fingers of my other hand on the inside to gently coax the clay wall outward in just that spot. The clay thins as it stretches, and you learn to anticipate where to leave the necessary extra clay when you pinch out the coiled walls. As I move clay and change the form, I'm constantly judging the thickness of the clay wall between

Christyl Boger,
Couplet (Male), 2000
14 x 20 x 10 in.
(35.6 x 50.8 x 25.4 cm)
Coil-built white earthenware; electric fired, cone 6; commercial decals, gold luster, cone 018
PHOTO BY ARTIST

Christyl Boger,
Prima Matria, 2001
30 x 24 x 24 in.
(76.2 x 61 x 61 cm)
Coil-built white earthenware; terra sigillata, low-fire glazes, cone 04
PHOTO BY ARTIST

my thumb and fingers. The piece will be stronger if the walls are all of even thickness and compression. (If a spot becomes overstretched or thin, carefully add more clay to that area and smooth it in with a finger or rib, being careful not to trap air in the wall.) When I have the shape I want, I let the area firm up a bit, then gently compress both the inside and outside with a soft rib. Because I want to continue to move the clay wall from both sides, I try to maintain access to the interior of the form for as long as possible. If necessary, I'll cut into a finished area to get to the inside.

The hands and feet also start out as hollow pinched forms, with extra solid clay left in the finger and toe areas. After completing the basic shape, I close the opening with a little cap of clay, creating a "balloon" of trapped air inside. I can then manipulate the gesture of the appendage by gently squeezing and twisting the

form into the desired posture. The trapped air supports the walls of the form and keeps it from collapsing inward. When the part firms up, I remove the clay cap and use small modeling tools to shape the individual fingers and toes. To attach the part to a limb, the two openings are carefully matched and both surfaces scored and slipped. Air trapped anywhere inside the piece can cause breakage during firing, so in narrow areas I place a straw or a roll of paper in the join. It ensures an air passage between the parts and will safely burn away during the first firing.

The basic structure of the head is made the same way as the rest of the body, with the approximate shape of the features built up with additional small bits of clay. These are smoothed and blended with my fingers and small brushes, and the details modeled with small loop tools. It's important to become familiar with a wide variety of tools and the marks they make, rather than rely on one tool to do every job. Serrated steel wax-modeling tools remove clay more evenly than do loop tools and are excellent for refining and contouring. The shallow score marks that they leave can be gently smoothed over with a small rubber rib or soft brush. Rubber-tipped shaping tools come with a variety of nibs and are used like tiny ribs to shape and polish small areas. Small paint-brushes are also excellent modeling tools. They can be used to move tiny amounts of clay too small for the fingers or to apply subtle details with slip. For shaping I prefer short flats or brights, with bristles that are soft but firm. A flexible seamstress's tape is the perfect tool for measuring and comparing proportions, which should be checked throughout the building process.

The fanciful hair on my figures is one place where I always have fun. Other than some thematic elements that are planned in advance (in this case twigs and sticks), this part of the work is spontaneous. I start by closing up the head in roughly the shape of the hair, using a needle tool to perforate the entire surface. This allows air that might be caught under the loosely formed hair to pass into the interior. The twisted coil "locks" of hair are added directly to the slipped-and-scored surface, and a small brush is used to push the coils into shape and add the appropriate texture.

Christyl Boger,
*Domestic Object
with Fruit* (detail),
2000
PHOTO BY ARTIST

As it transitions from wet to dry, the working properties of clay change. Careful timing of various procedures is critical to success. For example, coil building requires fairly moist and plastic clay. But every so often, weight-bearing parts must be allowed to firm up, or gravity takes over. Detail carving is much easier on leather-hard clay than on the sticky, too-pliable surface of wetter clay. Slipping and scoring joins separate parts into one, but if their moisture content isn't fairly similar, then different amounts of shrinkage will eventually pull them back apart. Experience is the best teacher when it comes to learning how clay behaves at different stages. The physical demands of clay can be challenging, but practice in the skillful handling of the material leads to greater choice and richer forms of expression.

I use a strong low-fire clay body that's a slightly modified version of a recipe developed by my former teacher Brian Bolden. It fires to an ivory white. For an even whiter surface, I use a body developed by Vincent Burke. I've tried higher-firing clays but found that the added stress on the pieces was unnecessary. The surfaces and colors I prefer are readily attainable at low temperatures. Most of the glazes that I use are commercially produced and can be applied either with a sprayer or a brush. Each piece is fired multiple times, at successively cooler temperatures, in order to accommodate my various surface techniques. I fire glazes from 04 to 06, decals at around cone 015, china paints between 015 and 018, and metallic luster at 018 or 019.

No one makes his or her work in a vacuum, and I've always had the benefit of talented teachers and colleagues, supportive institutions, and encouraging family and friends. And while the process of making art can sometimes be difficult, in many ways the world itself is supremely generous to artists. Our time and place hands us a ready-made toolbox that includes all of the accumulated knowledge, ideas, beliefs, written history, material culture, and living experience of humanity. All we really have to do to make good art is keep our eyes and minds open.

Top:
Christyl Boger,
*Domestic Object
with Fruit,* **2000**
**24 x 20 x 20 in.
(61 x 50.8 x 50.8 cm)
Coil-built white
earthenware; electric fired, cone 04;
commercial and
computer-generated
decals, cone 014;
gold luster**
PHOTO BY ARTIST

Christyl Boger,
Chymical Object,
2001
**17 x 14 x 14 in.
(43.2 x 35.6 x 35.6 cm)
Coil-built white
earthenware with
terra sigillata,
cone 04**
PHOTO BY LINDA CORDELL

TECHNIQUE:
COIL+PINCH

Christyl Boger,
Couplet (Female)
(detail), 2000
PHOTO BY ARTIST

2 It's important that coils don't get too dry, so I make each coil as it's needed, from logs cut from the clay block.

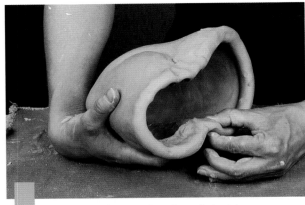

3 Coil building is an extension of pinching. Whenever possible I add wet coils to wet coils, relying on thorough pinching and ribbing to compress the join.

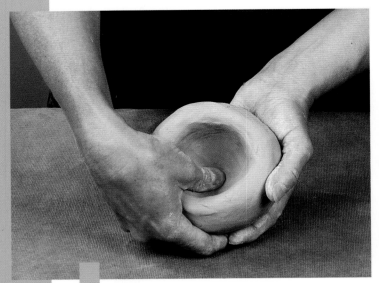

1 I always start with a pinched form and work from the ground up; since this piece will be a kneeling figure, the starting point is the leg.

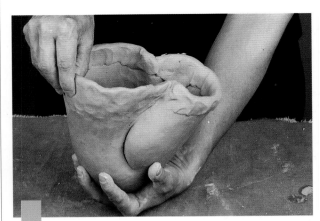

4 I shape the added coil carefully. The piece will be stronger if all the walls are evenly thick and evenly compressed.

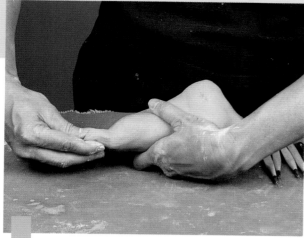

5   The foot starts out as a separate pinched form, with extra clay in the toe area for later carving.

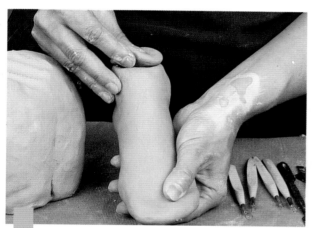

6   Trapped air supports the walls of the form while it's being shaped and detailed but the air passage must be reopened before attaching it to the leg.

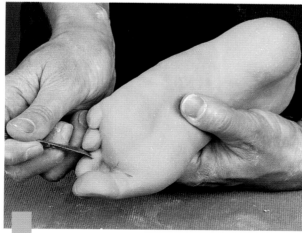

7   Small loop and modeling tools are used to shape the individual toes.

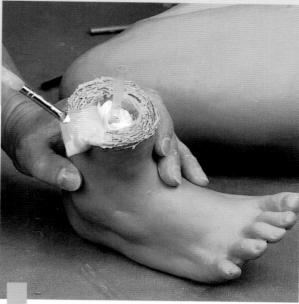

8   When joining these narrow parts there's danger of trapping air in the foot, causing it to break during firing. I use a straw in the interior to ensure an open air passage.

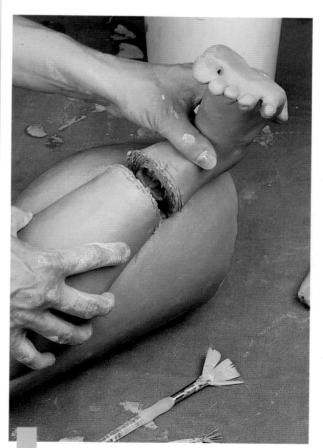

9   The foot is ready to be attached to the leg. The two openings have been carefully matched, and both surfaces scored and slipped.

10 Clay props hold the limbs in the correct posture and help support the weight of additional clay as the form grows taller. They'll stay in place through the first firing.

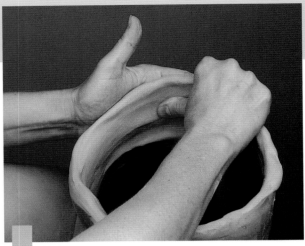

12 Shaping by pushing the form from the inside. Always support the piece from the opposite side when using directional pressure.

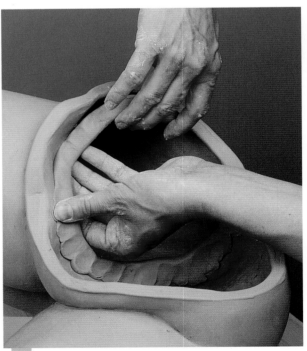

11 I use coils to join the legs and build the bottom part of the figure. Additional coils add extra thickness at the point where the upper leg joins the body at a crease. I'll deepen and refine this area later.

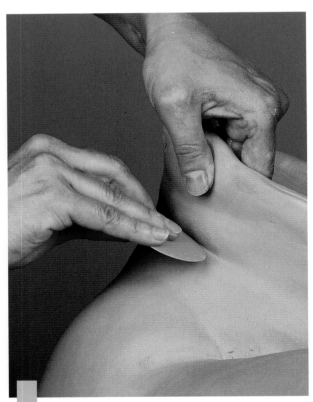

13 The edge of a rib is a versatile part of the tool. Remember to support the clay from the back but allow the clay to move in the process.

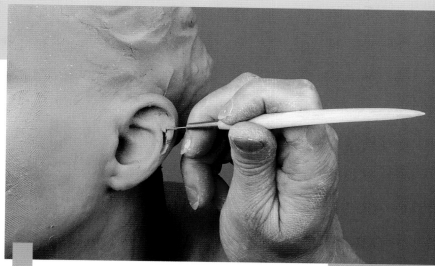

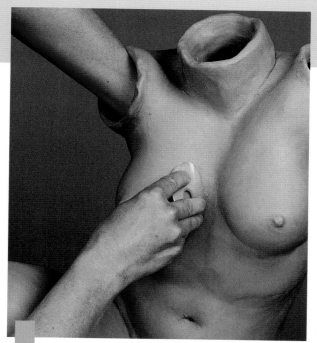

16 Small loop tools are best for modeling the hollows of the various features.

14 Any pressure on the outside of the figure must be matched with similar pressure from the inside.

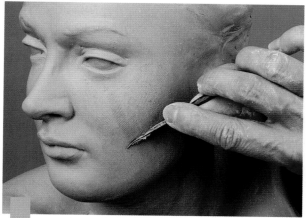

17 The long, serrated edge of a wax-modeling tool removes clay more evenly than a traditional loop tool.

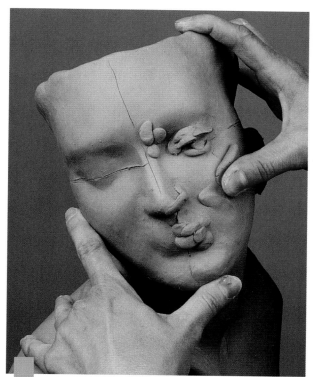

15 I start the face by building up the approximate shape of the features with small balls of clay. These areas are then blended with my fingers and small brushes.

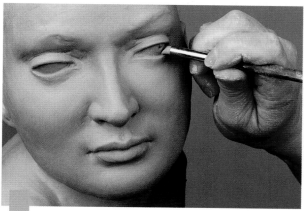

18 A rubber-tipped tool works like a tiny rib to shape and polish small areas. Here I'm compressing a smooth, round contour for the ball of the eye.

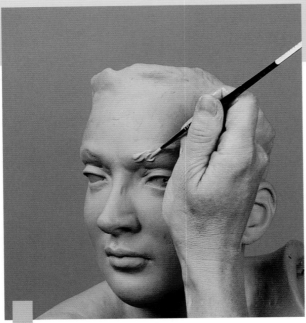

19 A small paintbrush applies tiny amounts of slip.

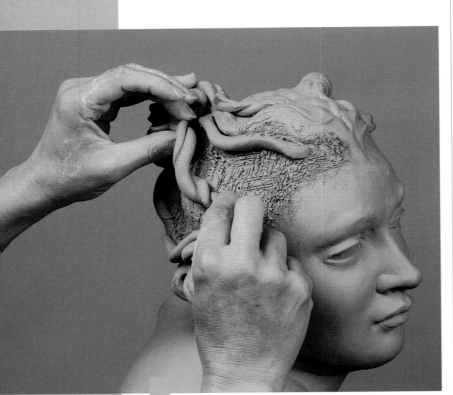

20 After slipping and scoring, I add "locks" of hair—actually loosely twisted sections of thinly rolled coil.

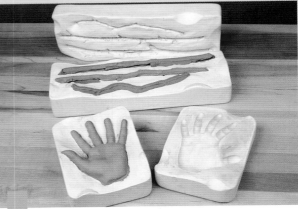

21 To create multiple small parts, and for found objects like these twigs, it's helpful to make a simple press mold. Now that I've taken the time to model this hand, I can use it for different figures by simply modifying the gesture.

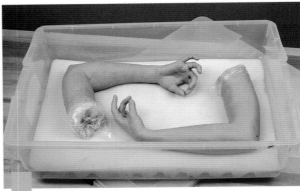

22 The arms and hands have been completed and are stored until they're firm enough to hold their weight in the raised pose.

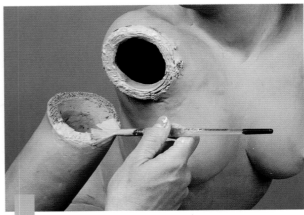

23 The openings of the arm and shoulder are carefully aligned, then attached by slipping and scoring.

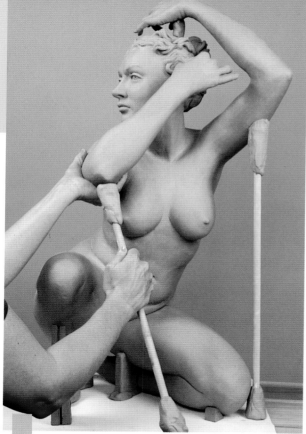

24 The arms need some support while the joined seams set up. I've padded the ends of the dowels with clay to help hold them in place and to allow for some movement as the piece starts to dry.

25 Small thematic and ornamental details are fitted and attached to the hair.

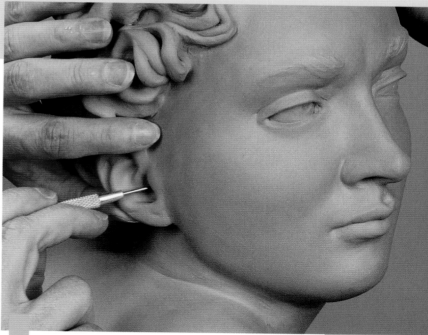

26 The deep cavities of the nose and ears are ideal for hiding air vents, as are the recesses of the hair and any surfaces that the figure rests on—in this case, the bottom of the right foot and the left leg.

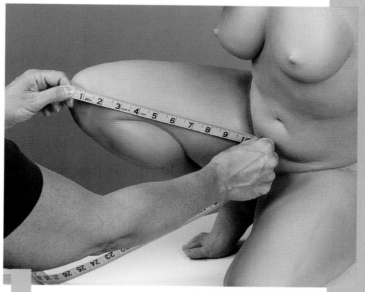

27 A flexible seamstress's tape is the perfect tool for measuring and comparing proportions.

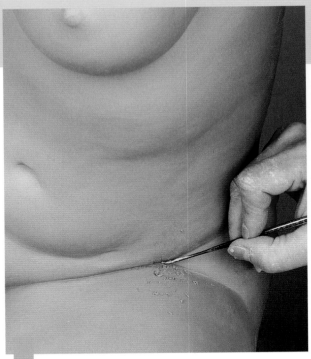

28 Once the piece is built, I refine areas of detail.

30 I use a soft rib to gently polish the slipped surface.

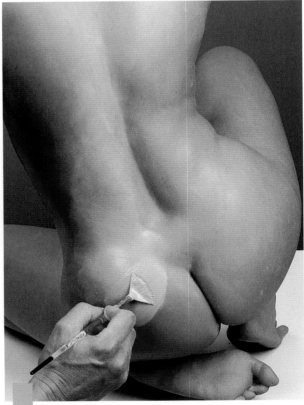

29 I apply several layers of fine slip, made from the same clay, to the entire surface.

LOW-FIRE WHITE EARTHENWARE

This recipe was adapted from one given to me by Brian Bolden. Fire to cone 04.

EPK	20
Tile 6 clay	10
OM4 ball clay	25
Gold Art clay	20
Talc	15
Wollastonite	10
Total	**100**
Add	
Bentonite	2–3
Molochite (white grog), fine or medium mesh	10–15
Handful of nylon fibers	

VINCE'S CADILLAC

Fire this white earthenware to cone 04.

OM4 ball clay	30
EPK	20
Tile 6 clay	10
XX Sagger clay	10
Flint	10
Talc	5
Ferro frit 3124	15
Total	**100**
Add	
Molochite (white grog), fine or medium mesh	10–15
Handful of nylon fibers	

Christyl Boger, *Brood XX*, 2004
32 x 20 x 20 in.
(81.3 x 50.8 x 50.8 cm)
White earthenware and glazes, cone 04; decals, china paint, and luster, cone 018
PHOTO BY ARTIST

GALLERY
OF INVITED ARTISTS

Linda Cordell, *split cock*, 2002
18 x 18 x 12 in. (45.7 x 45.7 x 30.5 cm)
**Slip-cast and hand-built porcelain; reduction fired,
cone 10; overglaze, cone 022; resin-coated top**
PHOTO BY ARTIST

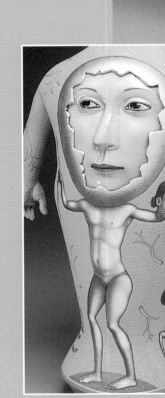

Jack Earl,
*Scraps and
Slats*, 2003
26 x 18½ x 11
in. (66 x 47 x
27.9 cm)
**Ceramic,
acrylic paint**
PHOTO BY TOM
VAN EYNDE
COURTESY OF
PERIMETER
GALLERY

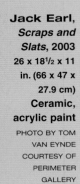

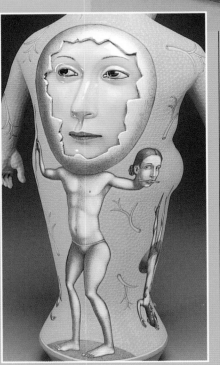

Sergei Isupov,
Ribbit, 2004
22 x 17½ x 9 in.
(55.9 x 44.5 x 22.9 cm)
**Hand-built porcelain;
electric fired, cone 06;
painted with colored
slips and clear glaze,
cone 6**
PHOTOS BY KATHERINE WETZEL.
COURTESY OF FERRIN GALLERY

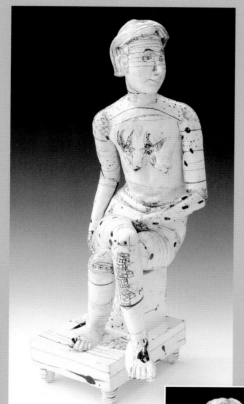

Sergei Isupov,
Ring of Fire, 2004
20 x 10 x 8 in. (50.8 x 25.4 x 20.3 cm)
**Hand-built porcelain; electric fired,
cone 06; painted with colored
slips and clear glaze, cone 6**

PHOTOS BY KATHERINE WETZEL.
COURTESY OF FERRIN GALLERY

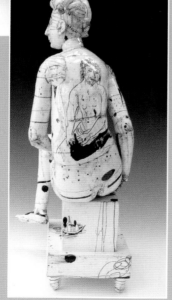

Philip Eglin, *Seated
Nude,* 2003
21 x 9 in. (53.3 x 22.9 cm)
Porcelain

PHOTOS BY TIMOTHY LOMAS.
COURTESY OF GARTH CLARK
GALLERY

Linda Cordell, *dissected dog,* 2002
13 x 21 x 16 in. (33 x 53.3 x 40.6 cm)
**Slip-cast porcelain; reduction fired,
cone 10; foam rubber gaskets**

PHOTO BY ARTIST

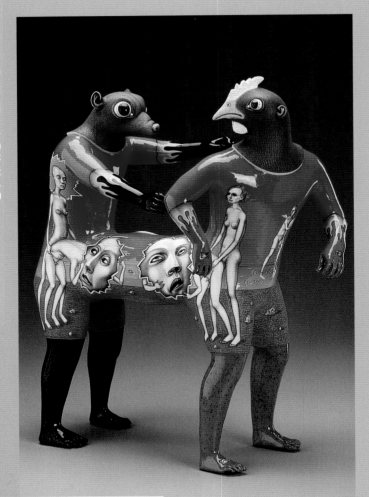

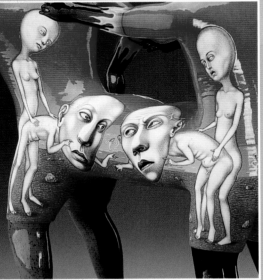

Sergei Isupov, *Doggie*, 2004
22 x 17 1/2 x 9 in. (55.9 x 44.5 x 22.9 cm)
Hand-built porcelain;
electric fired, cone 06; painted
with colored slips and clear
glaze, cone 6
PHOTOS BY KATHERINE WETZEL.
COURTESY OF FERRIN GALLERY

Michael Flynn, *Harewoman*, 2004
Height: 18 1/2 in. (47 cm)
Faience
PHOTOS BY RALF STOCKOFF

Christyl Boger

Laszlo Fekete, *Supermen's Mortal Combat,* **1999**
Height: 15½ in. (39.4 cm)
Porcelain
PHOTO BY TIMOTHY LOMAS. COURTESY OF GARTH CLARK GALLERY

Jack Earl, *The Old Story,* **1999**
12 x 8 1/2 x 8½ in. (30.5 x 21.6 x 21.6 cm)
Ceramic
PHOTO COURTESY OF PERIMETER GALLERY

Christyl Boger is currently a visiting assistant professor at Indiana University in Bloomington. She received her master of fine arts degree in 2000 from Ohio University in Athens. She originally trained as a painter and studied art at Miami University in Oxford, Ohio. Before returning to graduate school, she spent several years as the vice president of a special-events production company in Lansing, Michigan, and she credits this experience with giving her the real-world foundation that made it possible to pursue a career in art.

Ms. Boger first became interested in clay through an evening class at Michigan State University and soon began studying ceramics there full time. While in graduate school, she was asked to participate in an international sculpture sympo-sium in Germany, which involved completing a work for permanent outdoor installation in the city of Krosig. After com-pleting her MFA, she was awarded a summer residency at the Archie Bray Foundation in Helena, Montana, followed by the Evelyn Shapiro Fellowship at the Clay Studio in Philadelphia. In 2001 she began teaching at Indiana University and was recognized with an Emerging Talent Award by the National Council for Education in the Ceramic Arts (NCECA) in 2003.

Mark Burns
CERAMIC PASTICHE

CERAMIC METHODOLOGY AND PRACTICES REVOLVE AROUND A relatively small number of physical techniques that are the mainstay of ceramic manufacture. It's the individual artist who takes these "foundation" techniques and puts his or her own spin on traditional handling methods. I use basic slab elements, both hard and soft, to build my figural sculpture. These slab constructions are combined with castings from plaster molds, with great attention to surface detail, so that the final work is ubiquitous in its appearance and doesn't reflect the individual technical processes used in various combinations. The attraction of these simple physical processes is that they're easily married to one another in any given piece, and they often give the finished work the feel of having been lifted from only one plaster mold. I use the singular language of the cast object in its anonymity to separate the artist from the concept. The pieces stand alone as conceptual challenges and don't employ traditional "maker's marks" to signal how they were achieved. I'd rather have my work considered for what it is than how it was made. With careful planning, multiple clay bodies, varying firing ranges, and nonceramic materials can all be combined into one object. A piece may have as few as two or as many as a dozen ceramic processes involved, with parts made hours, days, or months apart. I rely on my vision to keep me involved and good planning to make the material work.

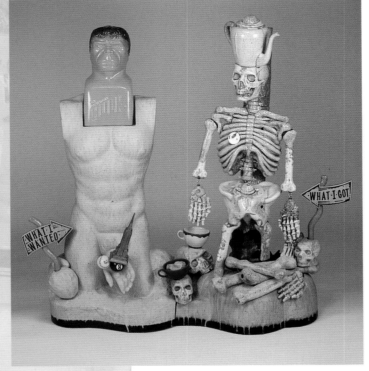

Mark Burns,
What I Wanted,
What I Got, 2000
48 x 48 x 22 in.
(1.2 x 1.2 x .56 m)
**Slab-built
stoneware/earthen-
ware with slip-cast
elements; electric
fired, cone 02; com-
mercial glazes,
glazes, cone 04;
china paint, decals,
cone 017; stainless
steel fittings**
PHOTO BY ARTIST

Mark Burns,
I, Monument, 1993
40 x 28 x 18 in.
(101.6 x 71.1 x 45.7 cm)
**Slab-constructed
stoneware with
slip-cast elements;
electric fired, cone
02; polychromed
surface; steel and
plastic elements**
PHOTO BY ARTIST

61

Mark Burns, *Mr. Coffee Nerves*, 2000
40 x 24 x 12 in.
(1 x .61 x .31 m)
Hand-built and slab-constructed earthenware with slip-cast elements; electric fired, cone 02; commercial glazes, china paint, cone 04
PHOTO BY ARTIST

The Ceramic Figure and Pop Culture

History, the mirror that reflects only backward, is a useful tool for the studio artist. Ceramics as a practice in the 21st century continues to use historical venues and ideas as a foundation for current practitioners involved in the ideology and visual/chemical/physical arrangement of clay as an art-making medium. The old adage that "those who refuse to learn from the past are doomed to repeat it" doesn't apply in light of the ongoing love affair between ceramics and the figurative artist. Serious ceramic artists certainly do learn from the past and are free to borrow from a long and rich history whenever and however they choose. Reinvention, not repetition, is the lineage for the use of the figure in clay. Observation of our ceramic history and its connection to humanist representation is not as complex as first glance would suggest. What we call pop culture, that sudden and most volatile of sociological whims, is actually an ancient practice that stretches back to the dawn of civilization.

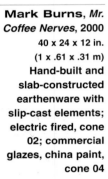

Make your own discoveries by trial and error. Invent. Risk.

Ceramics has an uncanny and basic ability to stop time, to freeze thought into static form through the manipulation of the artist and the truly astonishing physical characteristics of clay. More important, ceramics can coalesce the popular culture of many bygone eras into lasting increments on the yardstick of history. Pop culture is nothing new; rather, it's each generation's reassessment of historical/contemporary visual material filtered through a complex emotional reaction to the realities of any particular period of human existence.

Humans are narcissistic by nature; we enjoy looking at ourselves and at others. The ability of clay to capture not only the human form but also the human experience undoubtedly came quickly after the manipulative quality of the material was understood. It's important to understand that clay in its earliest manufacture was used in modeling figurines for magical or religious purposes long before it was used to make vessels. Figures, fetishes, gods, and monsters streamed through the fingers of unknown artists in our dim past, images frozen in clay to stand still in time. Unmoving as they may be physically, their power to move us emotionally has remained unchanged, as well as their ability to teach us something about the popular culture of their moment in time.

Without belaboring the point, it's certainly worthwhile to our investigation to understand that the marriage of popular culture and ceramics was inevitable. Ceramic figures are as eternal as humankind, and while not immune to the flux of current visual standards, they will never disappear. Ceramic material in the hands of the skilled artist can ensure that the figure will continue if for one reason only: we just like looking at ourselves.

Whether it be fact, fancy, or fashion, the representation of the human figure in clay and the realization that popular culture has always existed make it proper that artists will continue a long tradition of freezing time for generations to come. Their ability to discern meaning will certainly be colored by their ability to learn from history, whether a century ago or just yesterday. Perhaps the inevitable occurrence is actually that marriage made in heaven we so often hear about.

Thinking the Piece

As a practicing studio artist, I've long been associated with the figure as a springboard for visually complex ideas and situations. My work is an assimilation of many concepts and techniques brought together to engage the viewer. For me, clay is a material that can be forced into whatever shape or form I demand, pressed into service to realize the idea that engaged my curiosity initially.

For this piece I chose to focus my attention on what may be roughly described as "novelty" ceramics: those weird, impudent knickknacks, salt and pepper shakers, souvenirs of someplace you forgot you went, ashtrays, and lamps. Ceramic material has a long dalliance with light, from the earliest oil lamps of the ancient world to the familiar end table lamps you remember Mom having. The figure plays a prominent role in such objects, often using the light source as a dramatic gesture or whimsical touch. Of course, the apotheosis of novelty ceramic lamps came in the 1950s, when the outrageous was commonplace and the figure was at the height of its popularity as a decorative element.

The piece conceived for demonstration here incorporates several conceptual and technical processes. I began to pull seemingly unrelated material together, since blending wildly disparate elements into a single object is one of the hallmarks of my studio work. *Psychedelic Lollipop* is my favorite album title from the 1960s, the first album by the now defunct Blues Magoos. One wonders what might happen if such a lollipop was licked, and that thought was the inspiration for my piece. Sketches followed, and the final piece was determined: a boy, his psychedelic candy, and the wonders of mind expansion. The light elements in the piece give it the right "trippy" feel, and throwing the switch will give everyone who interacts with the piece a hand in making sure the boy is "turned on." I must admit to borrowing from Italian Capodimonte ceramic figural groups for the putti-like appearance of the boy and his bed of clouds. All the other physical gestures in the piece are strictly from the 1950s and the plethora of TV lamps I researched. Lengthy research was done into the physical structure of such an object, taking into consideration the non-ceramic elements that would have to be engineered into the final clay construction. The object presented was carefully thought out, since it incorporates three different clay bodies, each with its own purpose for the piece, as well as wiring, switches, plugs, and other hardware.

The concept in the beginning stages needed to be edited and shaped into what would become the final piece. For the techniques-in-manufacturing demands, I borrowed heavily from the novelty lamps of the 1950s in the physical appearance, surfaces, and glazes. There is a nod to the "fairy lamps" of the 1930s in the use of translucent porcelain as well. Many trips were made to electrical supply houses for materials, such as oddly shaped bulbs and appropriate switches that would blend seamlessly into the ceramic construction. Once the physical attributes of the piece were worked out and the correct nonceramic elements located, it was time to construct.

Mark Burns,
Old Queen Teapot, **1998**
24 x 22 x 10 in.
(61 x 55.9 x 25.4 cm)
Hand-built and slip-cast earthenware; electric fired, cone 03; commercial underglazes, glazes, cone 04; china paint, luster, cone 018; silk flowers
PHOTO BY ARTIST

Making the Piece

The piece was started with handmade slabs; no slab-rolling equipment was used due to the strain of particle alignment that is caused by intense pressure. Only the necessary slabs for initial building were rolled; afterward the pieces were made as needed. Throughout the construction, drawings of exact size were consulted as blueprints for the entire piece. To produce the shaped base, a slump mold was used with raw clay; the walls were of equal thickness.

Once the molded piece was firm enough to hold its shape, I released it from the mold and attached it to the foundation slab. The back was also attached at this time, demarcating the future height of the entire piece. Backboards and levels were used to ensure the proper angle of the back. Thus, a "stage" with finite edges was constructed, and the remainder of the piece was built within the stage.

Soft slabs, of equal thickness to the original construction, were rolled, cut, and eased into the piece to begin modeling a nongeometric form. As the pieces were

Mark Burns,
Space Headache Teapot, 1996
16 x 11 x 9 in.
(40.6 x 27.9 x 22.9 cm)
Hand-built and slip-cast earthenware; electric fired, cone 04; commercial glazes, cone 04; china paint, cone 018; stainless steel fittings
PHOTO BY ARTIST

added to the base, they closely resembled soft bricks, arranged so that no single seam ran continuously in any direction; this negated the possibility of running cracks during the drying process.

Once the modeled form was begun, it was raised in equal increments of height to keep the construction level and to prevent the edges from drying too much before new clay could be added. Note that great care was taken to allow the lower layer of clay to start firming up so that new weight added wouldn't collapse the entire piece. The equality of the wall thickness also ensured even drying as the piece was raised, and helped to stop warping and cracking. While sometimes unavoidable, I attempt to not use armatures of any kind inside my pieces. Since they don't dry out in the same manner or time as the outside skin of clay, they are quite visible once the piece is finished and bisqued. It's imperative for me to understand the physical attributes of my work from the inside out and to be able to predict what the fired results will yield. If armatures are used, they are spare and designed to hold the clay in place or bear weight for a short time only, until the natural strength of the material emerges through firing.

While the slab techniques were being used, the appropriate cast forms were simultaneously produced either by pressing or slip casting. These forms were released from the mold when firm and kept in a soft, leather-hard condition by being covered and airtight. I integrated them into the entire piece using scoring and joinery slips to mortar them into place. Again, I paid attention to the dryness and firmness of the previous construction to support new material.

Once the cloud arrangement was modeled into place, the slip-cast body was inserted into the construction, as well as the other cast forms that complete the design of the figure's body. At this time, apertures were made to accept nonceramic materials in the final processes of finishing, after all firings were done; shrinkage rates of the chosen body were taken into consideration so the openings would be the correct size after glazing.

The head of the figure was sculpted by hand in advance, from bulk clay, using traditional modeling tools.

It was cast in plaster, thereby eliminating the signature look of basic ceramic sculpting when translated through slip casting. It's important to bend all the processes used in the service of a singular style, to ensure that the finished piece has a homogenous appearance.

Small details were added by freehand modeling after the head was attached to the body. Previously fired porcelain shades were fitted into the construction at this time, in the same manner used for the nonceramic elements.

Details such as the lollipop were constructed separately for integration after glazing. The earthenware flowers around the base were made separately as well, and hidden glue "reservoirs" were cut into the base to hold the epoxy paste.

Once the figure was finished and the surface refinement accomplished to integrate all the processes into a singular surface, the piece was prepared for bisque. I cut open the back to allow electrical wiring to be installed at the end, and the aperture was engineered to allow a nonceramic covering to be attached at the final finish.

After construction was finished, I dried the piece carefully from the bottom up. The bottoms of my pieces dry first due to the way they must be built. Drying time can vary from two days to two weeks, depending on the complexity of the structure. I never rush or force-dry my sculpture using heaters, hot boxes, or stripping guns. All seams must heal naturally, using gravity to pull them together. Since so much care is taken to manufacture a piece with completely even walls, the drying process is usually quick, with no cracking.

Bisquing the object was standard, using Orton cones and taking the piece to maturity to give it lasting strength.

I used a commercially available manufactured glaze overall. I use such glazes literally as I would watercolors, eschewing the directions on the bottles and using my experience with them to guide me. Since I wish my work to carry material anonymity, I don't rely on self-manufactured glazes or self-produced clay bodies. While I do make glazes and recycle my clay, it would be foolish to espouse any one or two particular glazes or clay bodies as the only materials in my

Mark Burns,
B.J.'s Pipe Dream,
2003
20 x 12 x 5 in.
(50.8 x 30.5 x 12.7 cm)
Slab-built and hand-built stoneware/earthenware with slip-cast elements; electric fired, cone 04; commercial glazes, 1950°F (1065.5°C); china paint, cone 017; stainless steel screws
PHOTO BY ARTIST

repertoire. I use what is necessary to produce the objects I conceptualize, and the material used literally changes from piece to piece. Part of the interest I have in ceramics is finding the right elements to support my ideas and fitting them into my work. As you might suspect from the large amount of engineering needed, I often don't "see" the entire piece I'm working on until it's done. I rely on drawings and good judgment to pull disparate elements together in one cohesive piece. Once the glazing was complete, the fitted elements were glued into place, and in this case, all electrical work was done.

The work I produce is singular in the power that ceramic materials can evince, by being used to support (and not overwhelm) the ideas I have. What I would like and encourage you to take with you isn't so much technical as it is emotional. Be bold! We aren't married to any one process for a lifetime. Make your own discoveries by trial and error. Invent. Risk. Our collective ceramic history allows for however you choose to follow your bliss.

TECHNIQUE:
SLAB + CASTING

Mark Burns,
*Psychedelic
Lollipop* **(detail),**
2004
PHOTO BY SAM DAVIS

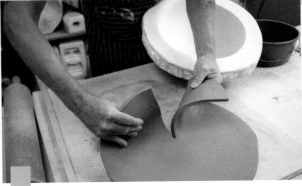

2 The base form is begun using a slump mold. The slab has been cut and darted to ensure a correct fit into the mold.

3 The slab is firmly pressed into place inside the mold.

1 The initial construction slabs are rolled; lath strips ensure even thickness.

4 Softening the clay with a wet sponge to ensure the clay can "stretch" evenly within the mold

5   For firmer attachment to the base slab, a thickening coil is added to the bottom of the pressed form.

6   The foundation and back slabs are prepared. The released mold form is altered before attachment to the base slab.

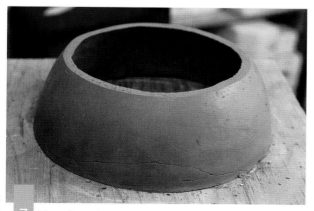

7   The altered mold form, cut to its proper height

8   The altered mold form is cut to fit the foundation slab.

9   Sizing the foundation slab for attachment of the mold form

10 The back construction slab is cut into its proper shape.

11 Preparing the back construction slab for attachment

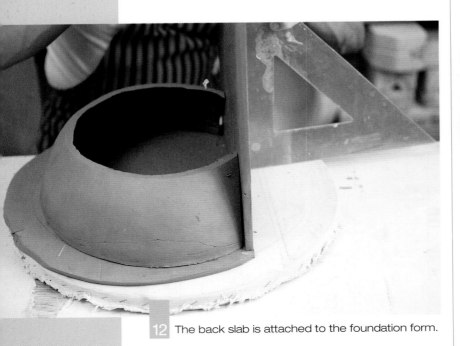

12 The back slab is attached to the foundation form.

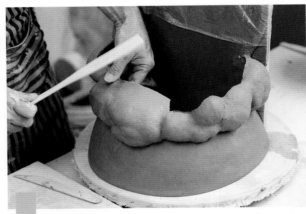

13 Using a soft-slab technique, the cloud form is built in equal height increments.

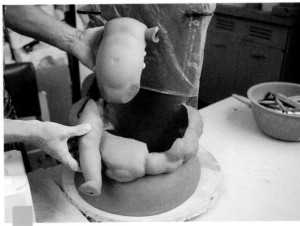

14 Paddling compacts the clay and strengthens the seams of adjoining pieces.

15 Assessing how much more cloud will be needed before the body can be attached. After removing all casting sprues and flanges, the cast leg will be fitted to the opening in the body.

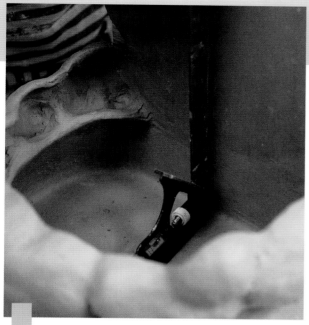

16 A level is used to check the angle of the back wall.

18 The piece is allowed to rest between additions of more clay, firming up to accept the new weight to come.

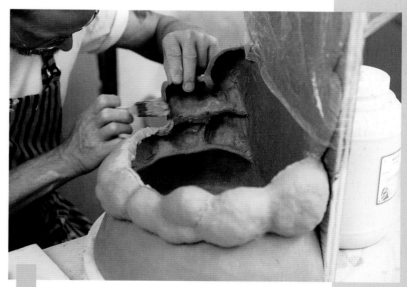

19 Raising the cloud another level and keeping the entire wall an even thickness

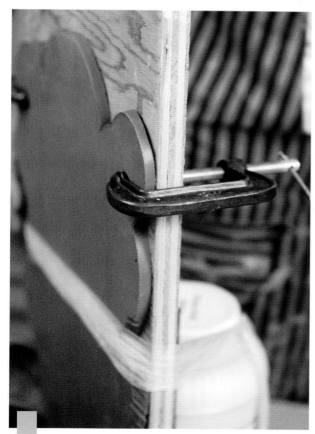

17 The back construction slab is lightly clamped to a backing board to stop it from falling forward.

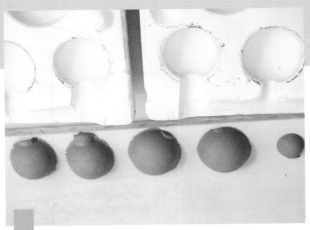

20 Cast forms are produced simultaneously with the slab construction for future additions to the form.

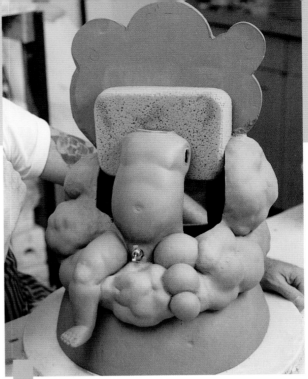

22 The figure is balanced so that it's parallel to the back wall of the construction. Note that the electrical switch is temporarily in place to test functionality.

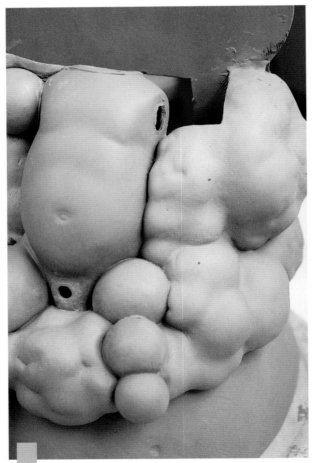

21 The cloud form is raised to new levels to allow for incorporation of the slip-cast figure body, made from a commercial doll mold. Note that an aperture has been allowed for the inclusion of electrical fittings later on.

23 Slip casting the head of the figure

24 Draining the head mold; its thickness matches the wall construction.

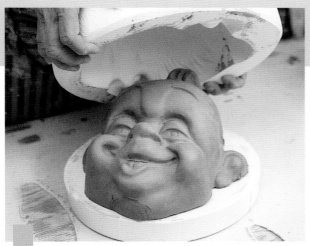

25 Releasing the head piece from the mold. The form was sculpted and cast as a plaster mold prior to beginning the entire construction.

27 Close-up of the head after its integration into the piece. The tongue was modeled freehand then added to the head.

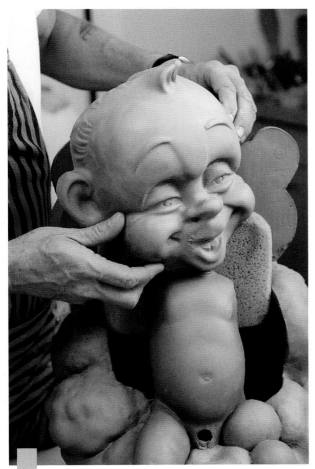

26 Sizing the head's opening to that of the body for attachment

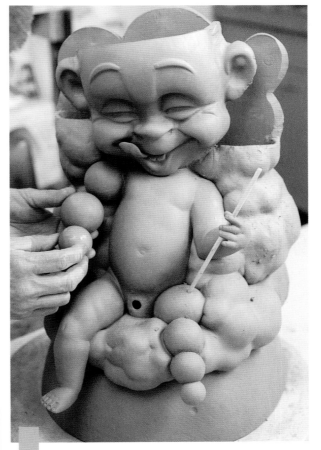

28 Fitting the forms of the arm to the figure. Note that on the right side of the figure, a dowel holds the place for a future part.

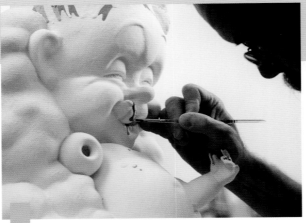

29 The piece has been finished and bisque fired. Glazing has commenced. The right arm of the figure was engineered so that it could be assembled after glaze firing.

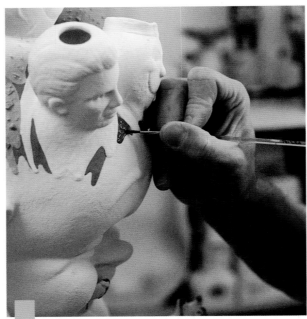

30 Close-up of glazing technique. The additional heads were either modeled or slip cast from molds made from simple plaster toys. Note that the open apertures will be able to accept electrical fittings and shades later.

31 These fittings will be added after the glaze firing. They include earthenware flowers, translucent slip-cast porcelain objects that will function as "shades" over some of the bulbs, and the electrical hardware.

32 Ensuring the proper fit of the porcelain "shades"

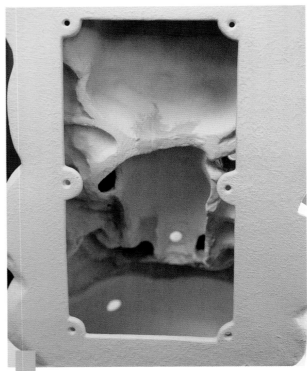

33 A detail of the construction's back, showing the allowances for the wiring and a fitted, nonceramic back panel that will be added after all the firings are finished.

Mark Burns,
*Psychedelic
Lollipop,* 2004
28 x 18 x 13 in.
(71.1 x 45.7 x 33 cm)
Stoneware, earth-
enware, porcelain;
cones 03, 04, and 6;
glass, metal, and
plastic additions
PHOTO BY SAM DAVIS

GALLERY
OF INVITED ARTISTS

Jason Huff,
Happy Birthday Santa Claus, 1998
30 x 14 x 15 in.
(76.2 x 35.6 x 38.1 cm)
Coil-built terra cotta;
electric fired, cone 04;
underglaze, glaze, luster;
flocking, bubble lights

PHOTO BY RICHARD NICOL

**Jack Thompson
(a.k.a. Jugo de
Vegetales),** *Cynara*, 1982
15 x 16 x 17 in.
(38.1 x 40.6 x 43.2 cm)
Slip-cast and slab-built low-
fire whiteware clay; gas
fired, cone 06; airbrushed
acrylic paint, matte clear
acrylic lacquer sealer

PHOTO BY ARTIST

Jason Huff,
*American Kings:
Don King*, 2000
7 x 3 x 3 in.
(17.8 x 7.6 x 7.6 cm)
Coil-built terra cotta;
electric fired, cone 04;
underglaze, glaze;
velvet, needles, pins

PHOTO BY RICHARD NICOL

Janis Mars Wunderlich,
Sport Utility Mother, 2004
22 x 12 x 7 in. (55.9 x 30.5 x 17.8 cm)
Coil-built and hand-built earthenware; electric, multi-fired, bisque
cone 3; slips, underglaze,
overglazes, Gerstley borate,
glaze cone 04–06

PHOTOS BY JERRY ANTHONY

Russell Biles, *Hero*, 2004
25 x 8 x 18 in. (63.5 x 20.3 x 45.7 cm)
Coil-built porcelain; electric
fired, cone 5; underglaze,
gold luster, clear glaze

PHOTO BY TIM BARNWELL

**Jack Thompson
(a.k.a. Jugo de
Vegetales),** *Catwoman
(Mujer Gata)*, 2002
36 x 45 x 13 in. (.91 x 1.1 x .33 m)
Press-molded and modeled
terra cotta and raku clay body;
gas fired, cone 01; unglazed

PHOTO BY ARTIST

Russell Biles, *U.S. Interest
(Fred, Daphne, Scooby,
Shaggy, Velma)*, 2002
Largest: 13 x 16 x 13 in.
(33 x 40.6 x 33 cm)
Coil-built porcelain; electric
fired, cone 5; underglaze,
clear glaze

PHOTOS BY TIM BARNWELL

**Janis Mars
Wunderlich,**
*Six Swans
(Bird Brain)*, 2004
20 x 12 x 12 in.
(50.8 x 30.5 x 30.5 cm)
Coil-built earthen-
ware; electric fired,
bisque cone 3; multi-
fired glaze, slips,
underglaze, Gerstley
borate, overglazes

PHOTO BY JERRY ANTHONY

Yvonne Lung, *Between a Rock and a Hard Place*, 2003
12 x 12 x 7 in. (30.5 x 30.5 x 17.8 cm)
Slab-built whiteware and porcelain; electric fired, cone 6 and cone
04; china paint, luster, decal, cone 016 and cone 019

PHOTO BY ARTIST

Mark Burns

Mark Burns received his BFA from the Dayton Art Institute, Dayton, Ohio, in 1972, and his MFA from the University of Washington, Seattle, in 1974, working with Howard Kottler and Patti Warashina. He has taught extensively since 1974, either full-time or as a visiting artist at many distinguished institutions. Among these are the Philadelphia College of Art, the Chicago Art Institute, and the Rhode Island School of Design. Mr. Burns is presently a full professor of art, head of the ceramics area, and chair of the Department of Art at the University of Nevada, Las Vegas. In addition to teaching, he lectures extensively and has been hosted by dozens of major schools of higher education over the past 30 years.

Mr. Burns has been the recipient of two National Endowment for the Arts fellowships and is the author of *Fifties Homestyle: Popular Ornament of the USA* (Thames and Hudson/Harper and Row, 1986). He worked for many years as the master modeler for G. Stewart Restoration Studios in Philadelphia, restoring major antique ceramics for the international trade as well as fine art for public and private collections.

Mr. Burns' work has been included in well over 100 exhibitions in major museums, both nationally and abroad, as well as in important private collections. Public institutions such as the American Craft Museum in New York and museums in Canada, Finland, the Netherlands, Japan, and Korea have collected Mr. Burns' art.

Yvonne Lung, *The Stepmother Devours a Pig's Heart (Which She Thinks Is Snow White's)*, **2003**
31 x 23 x 15 in. (78.7 x 58.4 x 38.1 cm)
Stoneware; electric fired, cone 04
PHOTOS BY ARTIST

Arthur González
FROM THE INSIDE OUT

MY WORK HAS ALWAYS BEEN ABOUT THE FIGURE, THE FIGURE

has always been about narrative, and the narrative is important to the figure. The figure has a job to do and he or she needs to be involved in it. This implies that the figure is sentient, that it has awareness. I've always maintained that my work has to embody more feeling than a simple statue.

Arthur González, *The Horizon Is Sitting beside You* **(detail), 2002**
PHOTO BY
JOHN WILSON WHITE

This, in a nutshell, is why the "inside-out method" is an appropriate approach for me. It's immediate and tactile. The tools used are your own 10 fingers and, consequently, the life of the piece is literally in your hands. This method holds great possibilities for invention. The figure emerges and what was once a piece of clay is now a person staring back at you. The face is brand new and doesn't "represent" anyone else.

**Arthur
González,**
*The Horizon Is
Sitting beside You,*
2002
52 x 27 x 13 in.
(1.3 x .69 x .33 m)
**Coil-built low-fire
red clay; gas fired
in reduction, cone
2; gold leaf, natural
sponge, rabbit's
foot, rope, horsehair**
PHOTO BY
JOHN WILSON WHITE

79

The Inside-Out Method

In time, technique breeds philosophy, which necessitates newer, more appropriate techniques. I've developed one that I call "same-time clay". It's a simple approach: fresh clay is attached to fresh clay, so that scoring and slipping aren't necessary. This basic approach to technique establishes a relationship with the clay that contributes to the belief system of the sculpture itself. Anthropomorphizing the art is an idea that you can find in Peter Voulkos's sculpture, as well as in the paintings of Jackson Pollack and Mark Rothko. I was first a painter who realized I was painting sculptural ideas, and when I switched to a focus of sculpture, I did so with the philosophy of a painter. That's why my work is predominately wall-oriented; it has the language of painting translated into the language of dimensional form.

The inside-out method of clay sculpting is one that enables you to create sculptural forms that are, in essence, neither additive nor subtractive. Accessing the form's interior volume, you can, without adding more clay, achieve most of your desired results by moving the wall of the form, pushing the clay out from the inside and in from the outside. This method requires a moderate-grog clay body (I use Quyle's red) that's also elastic enough to take the pushing and stretching of the clay wall. One advantage of this method is that the end result has a natural, skinlike appearance. I prefer to create the form in this way because my hand can modify the clay wall much like bone or muscle influences the look of skin, and I can circumvent the more traditional additive and subtractive methods, which have a kind of stereotypical look I want to avoid.

Another benefit of not adding clay parts (i.e., a nose, ears, or lips) to the form is that pieces won't pop off in the firing process due to poor attachment.

Making a Head

I'm going to demonstrate how to build a life-size head that starts in an upside-down position. First, I made a puki, a tool used by Native Americans to form a pinch pot. Typically, a puki is a shallow, fired bowl used to keep the bottom of the pinch pot round while holding the entire pot in shape. The traditional puki isn't strong enough for some larger forms and it also tends to be too wobbly, so in my interpretation it looks more like a leather-hard dog dish, pounded into shape with the heel of my hand, with slanted sides that make it stable and strong.

Once I've made the pinch pot, I stand it so that its bottom can be viewed as the cranium. I turn and hold the shape until I find a likely face, one that will slowly emerge through the rest of the process. To create a convincing face, one must have an understanding of basic facial structure. There are many good books, but the best teacher is your own awareness when you look at other faces—even your own. The fundamental approach is this: I set the head so that the side that promises to be the face is oriented toward me. This method lets me create the facial features in somewhat the same

Arthur González, *Good Thief, Bad Thief*, 2000
96 x 50 x 15 in.
(2.4 x 1.3 x .38 m)
Coil-built low-fire red clay; gas fired in reduction, cone 2; blown glass; epoxy, gold leaf, oil paint, engobes, mirrored glass, wood
PHOTO BY
JOHN WILSON WHITE

order that one typically perceives and visualizes them, from eyes to mouth.

Establishing the Terrain of the Face

Before I embark on the parts of the face, I need to establish the terrain of the face itself, its hills and valleys, so to speak. You may want to first decide on the gender and age of the face you're about to make. Personally, I like to make it up as I go and discover the new person as he or she emerges. If you're new at making faces, perhaps you should use a mirror. Keep in mind that no face is perfectly symmetrical.

I use one hand to massage the inside of the vessel by stroking it lengthwise with your fingertips, creating the cheekbone and, consequently, the lower half of the head and the mandibles and jaw. I make sure to use a stroking technique; if I simply push out with my fingers, I may break through the clay instead of stretching it.

What kind of nose will this person have? I gently bring the nose out of the thickness of the clay, remembering, though, that at this point I'm simply mapping the terrain of the face and not its specifics. I periodically evaluate my progress. Do you sense a person being born?

The Eyes

Obviously the face is made of countless variations, and that's why we all look different. There are no rights and wrongs with the face; however, for the sake of instruction, I'll talk in generalities for a moment. I use a fettling knife to lightly indicate on the clay's surface the placement of the eyes, making sure they're on the same horizontal plane and also that there's approximately one eyeball's-length distance between the two. I complete the work on one eye at a time and remember to work on the head's right eye first because I'm right-handed. Otherwise, my active hand will block my view of the first completed eye as I work on the second one.

Now the eyes are hollow and look like many classical Greek sculptures (although those originals once had painted eyeballs). I create a realistic illusion of eyes

and their whites using the teachings from Renaissance artists like Michelangelo, who in his sculpture created believable eyes with the use of negative and positive space. Whites don't need to be painted white to be convincing.

Whatever the type of eyelid, whether it has a heavy or hooded upper lid, or a thick bottom one, I continue to add appropriate details as needed. I believe that a fingernail (any length) is the best natural tool to fashion the hair for the eyebrow. Using a fettling knife or pin tool will make it look more like sgraffito, not hair on skin.

The Nose

Noses are actually quite fun. They can be simple or detailed, understated or prominent. I realize now that when I first began making noses I was idealizing them and not really understanding the subtleties of the bridge, the bone structure between the bridge and the tip, or the length and distance that the nose extends out from the face. Other things to consider are how nostril sizes and shapes relate to, and are in proportion to, the skin around and separating the nostrils, as well as the distance to the upper lip.

Arthur González, *The Skin Game*, **1997 48 x 70 x 9 in. (1.2 x 1.8 x .23 m) Coil-built low-fire red clay; gas fired in reduction, cone 2; cowhide, epoxy, glaze, engobes, yellow pollen**

PHOTO BY JOHN WILSON WHITE

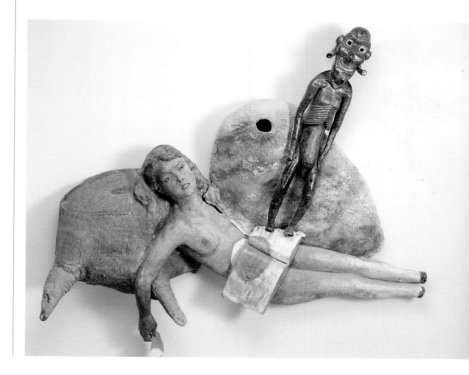

When you're making the nostril holes, it's also important to pay attention to the side view. The profile of the nose is connected to the profile of the lips and chin. In fact, it's not too late to extend your consideration more to the north. The profile of the nose begins with its bridge. When looking at a profile, I note the distance from the bridge to the eyes. I realize that a high bridge creates length without making the nose look overly long. Also, if the space between the base of the nose and the upper lip is very short, it can be the kind of classic nose seen in paintings by artists such as John Singer Sargent, whose aesthetic and cultural influences helped him decide that this was a profile of elegance. The interpretation of a type of nose or ear or mouth is always a subject for debate, determined by culture and generation.

I pay attention to the nostril's shape as it relates to the overall nose; many are actually oblong or ellipti-

cal. All noses have a particular angle and direction of pointing. If I'm trying to create the likeness of a living face, the nose can be the determining factor in making a convincing likeness. This is rather ironic, since we spend most of the time staring at people's eyes and mouths. As I study the nose's profile, I note the relationship of the nostril to the skin between the nostrils, and how much of the nostril hole you can see at that angle. Is it virtually invisible or still noticeable?

The Mouth

To make the mouth I must first establish its location. There's a piece of skin between the nose and the mouth with a small indentation and a certain length. This length is another important element of character identity. I must establish this indentation on the face before fashioning the mouth itself. With one finger, I simply press it in.

Next is the beginning of the upper and lower lips. You may have noticed by now that I don't use many ceramics tools. The more I rely on the natural facility and transformative abilities of my hands and the less I rely on my tools, the more empathy I feel for my subject. Once I know the general location of the mouth, I'll establish the lips. In doing so I've learned to look at my index finger in a completely different way, because it's the tool that will, in one quick gesture, create the beginnings of the upper and lower lips. Look closely at the end of your index finger and imagine that it's a lip-making tool. It has two sides: the nail and the pad; it's a sort of hoe! Think of using your finger as a two-sided tool to hoe a row in the clay face as long as a mouth is supposed to be. The result of the action will be the beginnings of two lips.

As you recall, the inside-out method doesn't involve adding any clay. Typical problems when sculpting the mouth are too-full lips (from added clay) or too-small ones (in trying to avoid creating a big mouth). Often, the result is what I call the "pucker effect". When in doubt, I make the mouth wider, but don't add clay. As I create the upper lip, I can realize greater fullness by carefully depressing the clay around the lip. The

Arthur González, *The Legacy of Cara Triste*, 2000
34 x 24 x 11 in.
(86.4 x 61 x 27.9 cm)
Coil-built low-fire red clay; gas fired in reduction, cone 2; blown glass, gold leaf, epoxy, engobes, whiskey
PHOTO BY JOHN WILSON WHITE

fullest area of the lips is in the center, and the corners are less fleshy.

Now I turn to the sides of the face. The cheeks are flexible sections of skin that hang off the cheekbone and are used to help eat food, speak language, yawn really wide, and blow balloons. Every little part of the face has a job to do, and that job defines its form and placement. I ask myself whether my sculpture looks like it has enough cheek skin to open its mouth if it needed to. Sometimes we get caught up in establishing the credibility of the obvious parts like the eyes, hair, and mouth, but there's a certain level of verisimilitude that must be attained in areas such as the cheeks, forehead, and chin.

The Chin and Jawline

Before addressing the chin, I look once more at the profile. What configuration are the nose, upper lip, lower lip, and chin going to have? A kind of consciousness can enter into the process of making faces as I realize that it's the unique combinations of these four parts that establish character and personality assessments. A long nose with a small mouth and weak chin has a completely different impact than a more "determined" chin or a "less obvious" nose. These phrases that we use to classify a face and its parts are very telling.

Once the chin is created, I turn the head to a profile once more. With hands placed inside and outside, establish the jawline. It's common for a first-timer to make a too-large jaw. Look in the mirror and notice just how subtle it is. Also notice how far back the jawline actually is. Even a very prominent jaw is a relatively short distance to the neck. The two most common perceptual errors are made in that distance and the one between the chin and ears.

The Ears

As with many aspects of naturalistic sculpting, the first challenge with ears is how to establish their location. The way that I find their rightful place is to plot two lines on the side of the head. The jawline estab-

Arthur González, *What Tool Must I Use (To Separate the Earth from the Sky)*, 2003
52 x 27 x 13 in. (1.3 x .69 x .33 m) Low-fire red and white clays; gas fired, cone 02–2; horsehair, rope, gold leaf, wood, wire, blown glass, glaze
PHOTO BY JOHN WILSON WHITE

lishes the vertical axis, and an imaginary horizontal line extends from the point of the cheekbone that's directly under the eye. The point at which these lines cross is the natural position of the ear.

Perhaps the best example of the inside-out method is the way that an ear can be made just by grasping some clay at this point. Don't forget the earlobe, either. The little bump in front of the ear hole is called the *tragus*. Without it the whole ear would look odd.

So far I've been concerned with the realism of things, but the inside-out method can be used also for non-realistic, nonfigurative, and nonobjective forms; it's truly as limitless as the imagination of the artist. That being said, the ear is a funny-looking abstraction

The narrative is important to the figure.

when I look very closely at it. Sculpting an ear is a matter of conveying believability, not necessarily realism, since most people aren't familiar with the visual maze of forms that makes up the outer ear.

**Arthur
González**,
Saging, 2003
28 x 60 x 18 in.
(.71 x 1.5 x .46 m)
**Low-fire red clay;
gas fired, cone 3;
wood, enamel paint,
slate, horsehair,
paper, antler, twine,
epoxy**
PHOTOS BY
JOHN WILSON WHITE

my hand. You can't make a mistake with hair because it comes in all forms (and often has a mind of its own). I work in locks of hair or, as when sculpting a bushy tree, break the entire form into clumps. I'm not afraid to dig deeply for those negative spaces. I think of hair as being groupings of forms, and don't try to make every single hair—certainly I never use a garlic press!

Completion

This piece was fired at cone 2 in an oxidation atmosphere. Oxidation maintained the clay's warm orange tone and brought out various subtleties in tone and chroma. I used Quyle's red sculpture mix, which reduces quite well. However, because I used many dark oxides on the surface, I didn't want to muddle the surface color by subjecting the clay body to reduction and consequently negating the brushwork.

Having completed the sculpting process I hold the head up one last time and ask the question, "And who might you be?"

Hair

Yes, believe it or not, this person will have wavy, medium-length hair without adding clay. If you recall, I made sure when I made my pinch pot to add a lot of clay on the bottom. I push the clay out from the inside while combing the hair with a raking action of

TECHNIQUE:
COIL

Arthur González,
Golden Girl (detail), 2004

PHOTO BY JOHN WILSON WHITE

1 I prefer a large-coil technique, making sure the walls of the pot are $^3/_8$ to $^1/_2$ inch (.95 to 1.3 cm) thick. Using a leather-hard puki made of clay, I press each coil firmly into the clay below it, creating an egg-shaped form. Too-thin walls compromise the strength of the form, so it's better to err on the side of too thick. I make the bottom of the pot $1^1/_2$ inches (3.8 cm) or more thick because I'll need this clay for hair later.

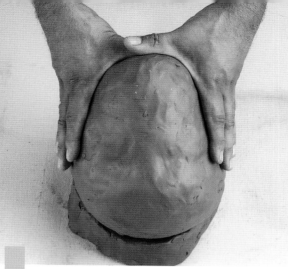

2 I grasp the head in such a way that my hands can shape a jawline.

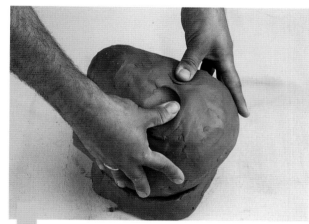

3 Depressing the clay to make eye sockets. I've noticed that a person's eyes are approximately halfway down from the top of his or her head. I make sure to allow plenty of space for the brain!

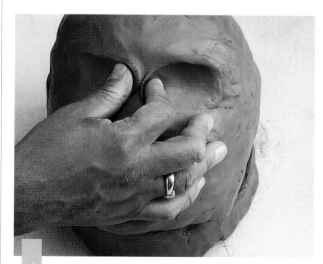

4 Establishing the general location of the nose and mouth. I pinch between the eyes to establish the bridge of the nose, which is a very important part of the face. It establishes the depth of the eyes and the prominence of the brow bone as well as the personality and age of the face.

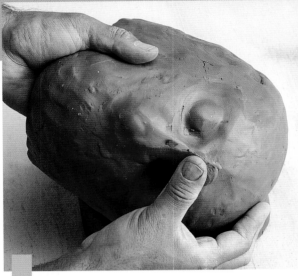

5 Before deciding on the type of eyes, I create eyeballs by pushing clay out from the eye sockets.

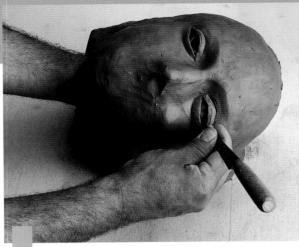

8 ...and pressing it into the eye socket where the eye white is to be. What direction is the face looking?

6 Supporting the eye area from the inside, I cut out a fish shape so that the top lid is larger than the bottom one.

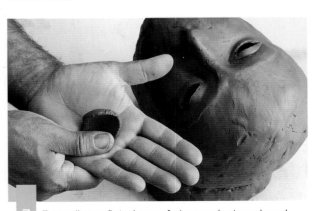

7 Rounding a flat piece of clay against my hand...

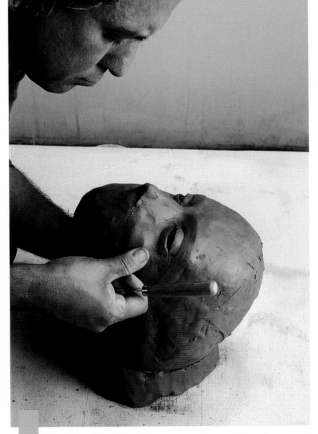

9 Continually adjust the proportions of the face as I refine each new feature. Bring out the cheeks by using short strokes from the inside of the head with the three fingertips of my index, second, and third fingers.

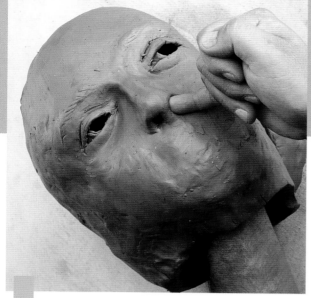

10 Using my fettling knife and then my little finger to create a natural edge to the nostril.

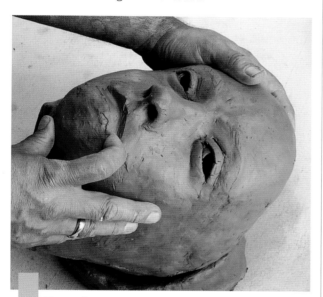

11 The nail creates the upper lip and the pad of my finger will create the bottom.

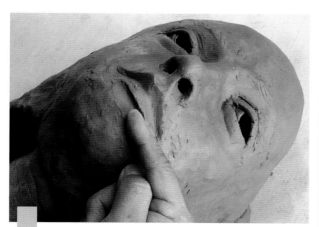

12 Before shaping the bottom lip, I create its thickness by simply depressing the clay slightly under the lip.

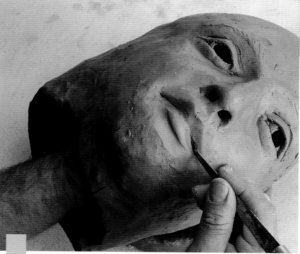

13 Finishing sculpting the bottom lip by depressing the clay around it and slightly depressing the corners of the mouth. This creates greater believability as to how the lips actually go into the mouth.

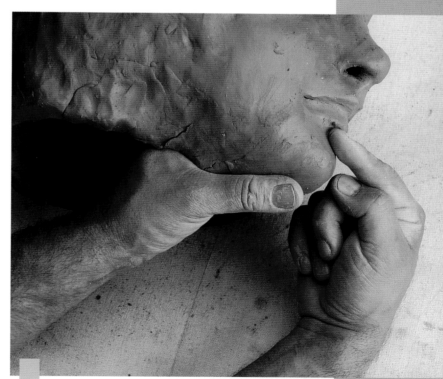

14 Once I decide on the chin's type, I bring it out from the face by pinching the clay underneath the chin. The degree to which the chin can be extended is determined by the thickness of the clay wall; I resist the impulse to add clay.

15 Again, I assess my progress.

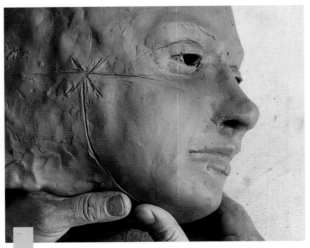

16 The ear is located at the intersection of two imaginary lines that extend from the top edge of the jawline and a horizontal extension of the cheekbone under the eye; X marks the spot.

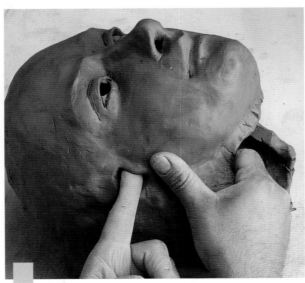

17 The hole of the ear (the external acoustic meatus) is perhaps the easiest thing to make; I just stick my thumb into the X.

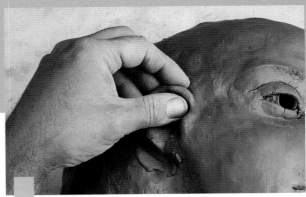

18 Once I've determined the size of the ear, with one hand inside the head for support, I simply grasp some clay for the outer ear and shape it.

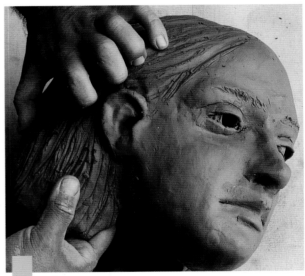

19 Using the excess clay that is still in the bottom (the cranium) of the form, I push, rake, and smooth it into a semblance of hair.

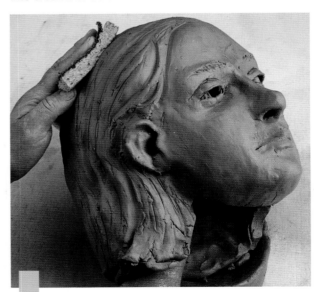

20 Using a damp sponge to naturalize the effect by blending all the locks of hair into a unified form. Now all of the parts relate the whole in a believable fashion.

Arthur González, *Golden Girl*, 2004
17 x 16 x 10 in.
(43.2 x 40.6 x 25.4 cm)
Coiled and pinched terra cotta, electric cone 2, oxidation; underglazes
PHOTO BY JOHN WILSON WHITE

GALLERY
OF INVITED ARTISTS

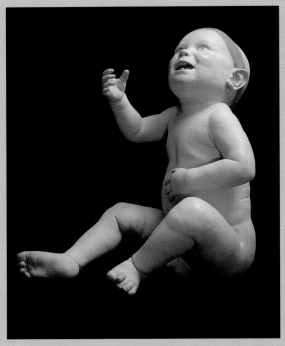

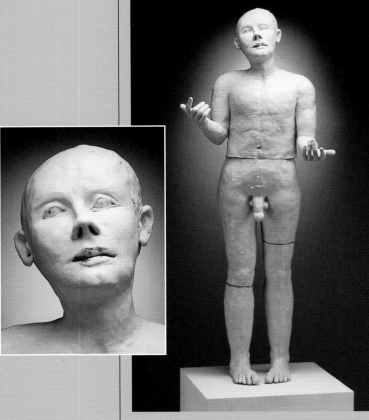

Judy Fox, *Friar Tuck*, 1995
18 x 12½ x 13 in. (45.7 x 31.8 x 33 cm)
Terra cotta, casein paint

PHOTO BY ARTIST. COURTESY OF PPOW GALLERY

Louise Radochonski, *The Calling*, 2004
65 x 19 x 19 in. (1.7 x .48 x .48 m)
**Coil-built and pinched stoneware; constructed
on metal armature; fired in oxidation, cone 6**

PHOTO BY WALKER MONTGOMERY

Robert Brady, *Quest*, 1995
25 x 10 x 15 in. (63.5 x 25.4 x 38.1 cm)
**Earthenware, glaze,
cone 06; sandblasted**

PHOTO BY SCHOPPLEIN STUDIOS

Judy Moonelis,
Magnetic Touch, 1998
84 x 9 x 9 in. (2.1 x .23 x .23 m)
**Pinched low-fire white
clay; electric fired, cone
02; steel pins, magnets,
steel, copper, brass,
found objects**

PHOTO BY ARTIST

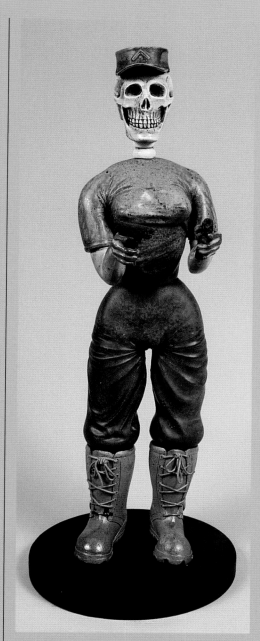

Gina Bobrowski,
Of Geography and Animal Dreams,
1997–2002
29 x 67 x 26 in.
(.74 x 1.7 x .66 m)
Ceramic, copper, steel, moss, lavender, rose and chamomile flowers, compasses

PHOTO BY WILLIAM TRIESCHVOELKER

Joe Bova, *American Daughter,* 2003
27 x 10 x 11 in. (68.6 x 25.4 x 27.9 cm)
Altered wheel-thrown stoneware and porcelain, sculpted and assembled; fired in reduction, cone 10

PHOTO BY MICHAEL SMITH

Judy Moonelis,
Touch Portrait (Elizabeth), 2000
68 x 18 x 6 in. (1.7 x .46 x .15 m)
Pinched porcelain; electric fired, cone 7; oxide washes, underglazes, wire, paper, plastic, encaustic, copper, steel

PHOTO BY ARTIST

Judy Fox,
Court Lady, 1999
$50^1/_2$ x 14 x 11 in.
(1.3 x .36 x .28 m)
Terra cotta, casein paint

PHOTO BY ARTIST. COURTESY OF PPOW GALLERY

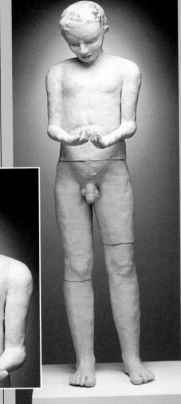

Louise Radochonski, *Standing Youth*, 2004
63 x 19 x 19 in.
(1.6 x .48 x .48 m)
Coil-built and
pinched stoneware;
constructed on metal
armature; fired in
oxidation, cone 6

PHOTOS BY WALKER
MONTGOMERY

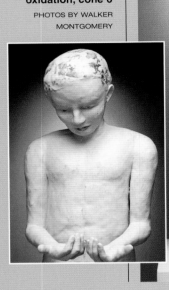

Gina Bobrowski,
Reservoir, 2001
50 x 22 x 13 in. (1.3 x .56 x .33 m)
Terra cotta, wood, coin, bone

PHOTO BY WILLIAM TRIESCH VOELKER

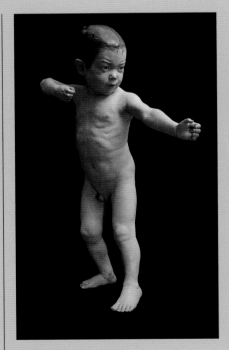

Judy Fox, *Attila*, 1996
31 ½ x 21 x 11 in. (80 x 53.3 x 27.9 cm)
Terra cotta, casein paint

PHOTO BY ARTIST. COURTESY OF PPOW GALLERY

Arthur González

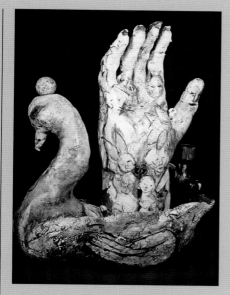

Gina Bobrowski, *Hand,* 2004
38 x 32 x 13 in. (96.5 x 81.3 x 33 cm)
Earthenware, wood, found objects
PHOTO BY WILLIAM TRIESCH VOELKER

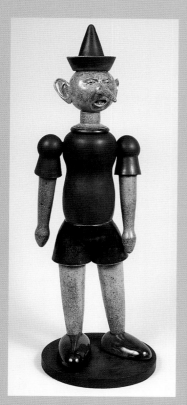

Joe Bova, *The Politician,* 2003
29 x 11 x 10 in.
(73.7 x 27.9 x 25.4 cm)
**Altered wheel-thrown
stoneware, sculpted and assembled; fired in reduction, cone 9;
salt glazed, cone 10**
PHOTO BY MICHAEL SMITH

Arthur González, a California native, received a BA and an MA from California State University in Sacramento before earning his MFA in 1981 from the University of California at Davis. His ceramic sculpture has been featured in numerous magazines and books, including *The Nature of Craft and the Penland Experience* (Lark Books, 2004). Mr. González exhibits extensively in both group and solo venues, and his art resides in many public collections, including the Allan Chasanoff Collection at the Mint Museum in Charlotte, North Carolina, and the American Craft Museum in New York. His creative work and teaching have been recognized by the Gerbode Foundation (2003) and the Warhol Foundation/Penland School of Crafts Artist-in-Residency Program (2001).

Doug Jeck
CLAY SKIN

THE ADVANTAGE IN SCULPTING WITH CLAY IS THAT THERE IS NO single technique. Because of this, working with clay is simultaneously liberating and daunting. Everyone who touches the stuff does it his or her own way. Give 20 people a ball of clay, simply ask them to stick their finger in it, and you'll witness 20 unique expressions. This isn't true for the woodworker, whose table saw cut or router gouge is indistinguishable from others'. Unlike wood or precious metals (a piece of expensive mahogany or an ounce of silver is wasted at great expense if improperly handled), clay is dispensable, cheap, and forgiving. If a work in clay should fail, squish it back into nothingness, or slake it down, remix it, and start over. This is not much of a hardship for small things—pinch pots, ashtrays, toy-size work. But when you are working with large-scale projects such as the figure involving months of tedious, delicate labor, the stakes are much higher.

Doug Jeck, *Study in Antique White*, 2002
54 x 60 x 40 in. (1.4 x 1.5 x 1 m)
Coil-built porcelain; electric fired, cone 4;
fabric, wood, hair, mixed media

The Sculpting Process

My ideas for generating and formulating a piece vary greatly. I never sketch or do studies for my work. The process is both conceptual and intuitive and therefore presents a unique paradox. Conceptually, I know that the thing that I make is just that—a thing. Even though it's a realistic human figure, it does not breathe, speak, feel, or think. It's an inanimate object and, because of this, is inescapably linked to the continuum of all human-shaped objects: statuary. Although I use the figure-pedestal format, which is conventionally reserved for important, heroic personalities, I try to subvert and dismantle the staunch, archaic canon of heroic figure sculpture, replacing arrogant Apollos or Caesars with anonymous nobodies like me. This is my general didactic framework. Intuitively, my work is a mess, and that's why I keep making it. My studio practice involves much more for me than simply manufacturing sculpture. The studio is my own private playground, torture chamber, dance hall, karaoke stage, and psychiatric couch. Things happen in there that nobody will ever see or know through the finished work.

The process photos in this chapter don't show it, but most of my studio time is spent listening to music (sometimes one track of a CD for hours), sitting and thinking about stuff that has everything and nothing to do with art, and looking intensely at the thing I'm making. Ultimately, I want the figures that I make to tell me as much as I insist that they say.

Working with clay is simultaneously liberating and daunting.

When I first decided to make life-size figures, I tried many different forming methods. By nature I'm pretty impatient and impulsive and I attempted many shortcuts. For example, I tried to lay big slabs of clay into 55-gallon (209 L) drum halves and construct them into people. I also made huge, solid mountains of clay into bodies and tried to carve them hollow, in the way that one might empty a giant, fossilized, human-shaped pumpkin. These techniques may work for some, but for me they were complete failures. The problem is that clay things that are larger than a grapefruit need to be hollow. If they're not, they blow up in the kiln; it's just that simple.

I asked myself, "Is there an advantage in making things hollow? Can a particular method be employed to create an object (specifically, a human figure), to offer more complex opportunities and information regarding content than would a mere adherence to the rudimentary, structural confines of the ceramic medium?" Yes, large figures made out of clay need to be hollow, but there is a symbolic corollary involved in this practice for me, which is why I continue to work with clay.

Essentially, I build a cavernous wall of clay skin. Symbolically, my figures are constructed in the same way that humans are: we all have internal and external pressures that define our persona, appearance, and psyche. When I construct and form a body, I have one hand on the inside and the other on the outside. Making the body in this manner is a negotiation between pushing from within and visually defining or tempering externally. No internal supports or armatures are used.

Once I built a figure and, when the clay was dry and stiff, filled it with plaster. I peeled off the clay to reveal the plaster evidence of the figure's interior—its soul. It looked like a maelstrom of sweeping, poking, punching, and tickling fingers, a sort of three-dimensional, corporeal seismograph. The interiors of all my works are no less than archival containers of this unseen energy. This is one reason why I build hollow figures out of clay.

My work takes a long time to make. I build the hollow human body by vertically adding 2-inch-wide (5 cm) strips of clay. Clay is rolled into coils (about the diameter of a bratwurst) and flattened into these $1/2$-inch-thick (1.3 cm), belt-sized strips. Rolling and flattening the clay compresses it for strength and flexibility. I then overlap the thin slabs and smear the seams together, creating a contiguous wall of well-tempered clay.

During the initial building process, I don't necessarily articulate the figure's details. Clay needs to get stiff in order to support successive vertical layers. If the figure that I'm building is standing, I start with the feet and may build up to the knee until gravity and the soft clay prohibit additional weight. At this point, I have the basic shape of lower legs and feet. Once the clay has stiffened, I can build more on top of it and continue to establish the details of the body. If one is conscientious about timing and the various stages of clay's workability (not doing too much too soon or too late), then any clay body is suitable for this technique.

I'm constantly working up and down the figure, realistically defining (through carving, brushing, and ribbing and smoothing) the lower, stiffer parts while waiting for newly added clay to harden.

This process is interesting because the lower features of the figure are more or less completed and defined before the rest of the body even exists. I don't use models, drawings, or maquettes; I just start building from the ground up. So the process is more akin to laying bricks and seeing a building evolve than it is to the traditional, subtractive method of sculpting an entire mass of material and seeing the figure's total form emerge from within. It's a process that's very much like writing a story—word after word, sentence after sentence, paragraph after paragraph. Each successive phrase that establishes character development builds on previous entries. In my case, knee considers foot, thigh considers knee, and ultimately the face's implied persona is the culmination (or, in some cases, the negation) of what the body's character demands.

Finding Persona

Establishing a face and an implied persona can involve weeks of work. I often cut off the head after

Doug Jeck,
Heirloom, **2000**
73 x 17 x 17 in.
(1.9 x .43 x .43 m)
Coil-built stoneware; electric fired, cone 4; hair, paint, wood, concrete, rope, pencil
PHOTO BY NOEL ALLUM

several days of working and begin again. Sometimes a face will show up immediately and be completed in a day or two. Searching for the "right" face to emerge is a nebulous, unpredictable process. As is true for the body, making the face and head involves pushing and stretching from the inside and the outside. I'm forming features, scratching lines, brushing, carving, pressing, squeezing, and looking for a complex personality to arrive. At a certain point, the head will suggest a psychological state that cannot be erased, and it's then pursued and refined.

There are no shortcuts or a magic wand to be waved over a clay head (or figure) to make it seem realistic. Although it's the most fun for me, defining features like nostrils, tear ducts, veins, lip wrinkles, cuticles, and so on is a painstaking process that takes many hours. I use dental tools, craft knives, dull pencils, and other small tools to carve and sharpen details—it's very much like drawing or etching in the round. A wet brush with porcelain slip is used to mute the carving lines, soften the details, and add a layer of smooth clay skin, hiding all traces of my tool marks. At this point, the clay is almost totally dry. I repeat this process until the piece resists any further attention. I know that I'm done forming a figure when I come to my studio, sit and look at the thing, and, after hours, cannot conceive of another move to make. Then I leave it to dry for the kiln firing.

My firing process is nothing special. I fire my work slowly in a very large electric kiln (fired once, usually to cone 2) and just keep my fingers crossed until I open the door and see that the piece has survived. A kiln is simply an appliance for me, and firing my work is not a spiritual endeavor but a necessity.

When the piece comes out of the kiln, I fill the legs with concrete to make it bottom-heavy and stable. The concrete sets around steel rods inserted into the legs through the feet. The steel rods protrude through the bottoms of the feet and are anchored into a cast concrete base so the figure and base are permanently attached.

Finishing

I usually finish my work with acrylic paint. Depending on the desired effect, I sometimes use spray paint, commercial patinas, hair, fabric, found objects, wood, fake plants, and other materials. Glaze is necessary only for pottery and food-safe items; there's too much chemistry involved for me, and it's unpredictable and therefore inappropriate to slather glaze over the months of intimate, detailed work invested in my sculpture.

When I paint, I use very thin successive washes of color that accumulate to give the depth and illusion of the transparency of skin. I try to establish a painted surface that doesn't look like it's been painted at all, but seems to emerge from within the figure.

Doug Jeck,
Cain and Abel, 2000
77 x 20 x 16 in.
(2 x .5 x .4 m)
**Coil-built
stoneware; paint,
concrete, plastic
foliage, wax,
hair, wood**

Doug Jeck,
Access, 2000
9 x 46 x 46 in.
(.23 x 1.2 x 1.2 m)
**Coil-built stoneware;
electric fired, cone 2;
hair, paint, wood,
burlap, blackberry
thorns**
PHOTOS BY MARK VAN S.

TECHNIQUE: SLAB

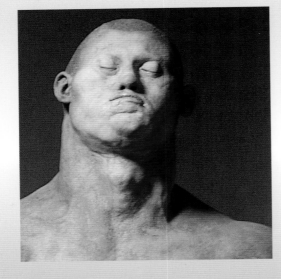

Doug Jeck,
John Henry
(detail), 2004

PHOTO BY REBECCAH
KARDONG

1 Rolling and flattening clay strips

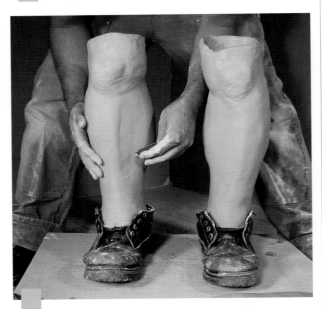

2 Building the lower legs

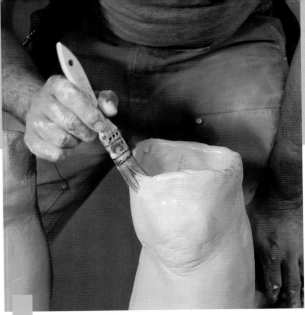

3 Wetting the edge of the hollow form for the addition of more wet clay

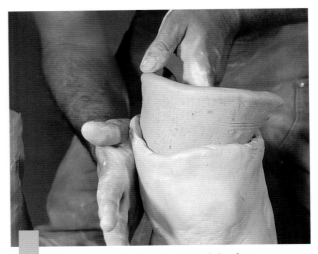

4 Adding strips of clay, to extend the form

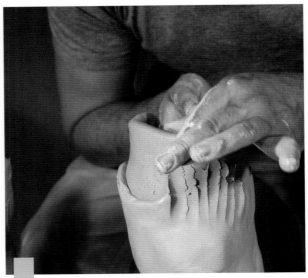

5 Adding flattened strips of clay and working them into the preexisting form

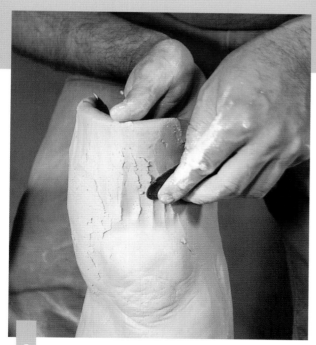

6   Using a rib to smooth the finger marks

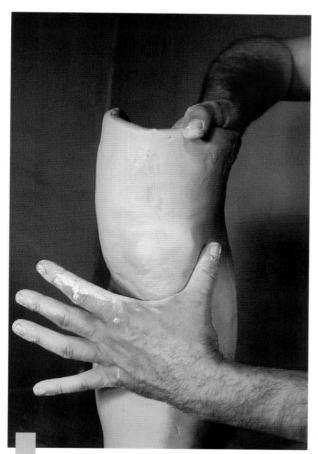

7   Smoothing the seams and initially shaping the legs

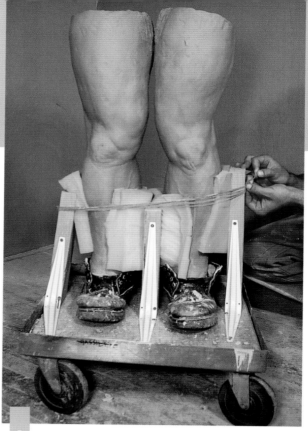

8   Reinforcing the legs on a cart with foam rubber, wood, and hardware

9   Preparing to join the thighs by scoring the clay

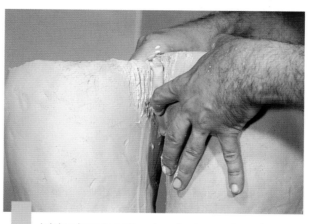

10   Joining legs together by slipping and scoring

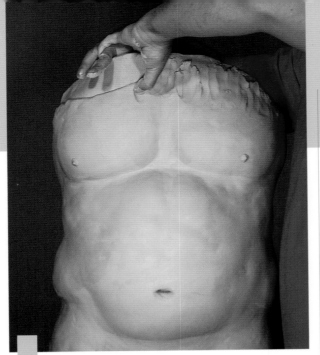

11 Continuing to build higher, adding wet clay to the stiff clay below

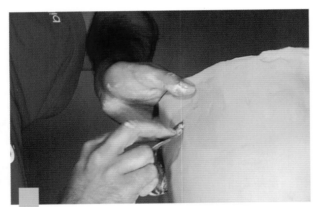

12 Ribbing and smoothing the clay and establishing the body's features

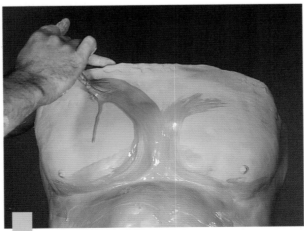

13 Adding porcelain slip and modeling with a brush to soften tool and hand marks

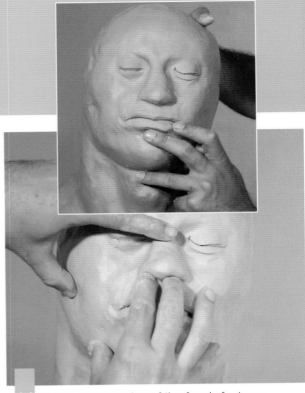

14 The basic formation of the face's features

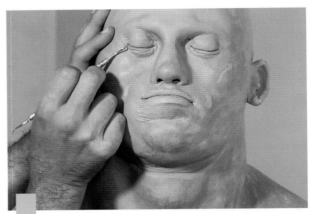

15 Refining the face's features with dental tools at the leather-hard stage

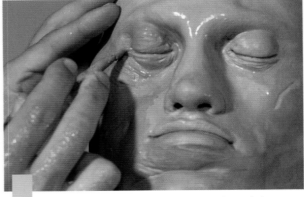

16 Using a small, wet brush to smooth and shape the face's features after carving

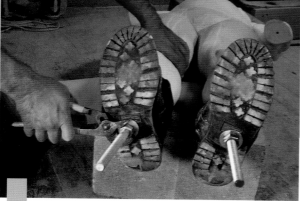

17 After firing, threaded steel rods are bolted into the legs, providing an internal armature that is then anchored to a cast concrete base.

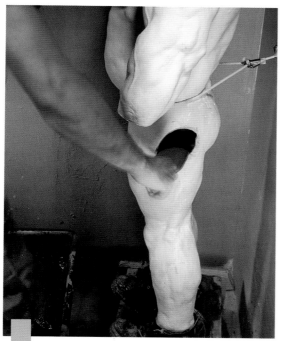

18 To add stability, the piece is filled to midthigh with concrete through holes in the legs, then mounted to a cast concrete base.

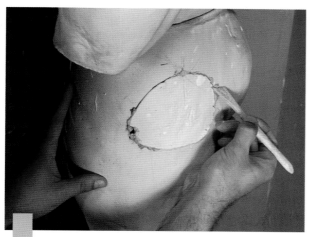

19 The holes in the legs are enclosed with the clay discs that were cut out during the green ware stage and sealed with epoxy putty.

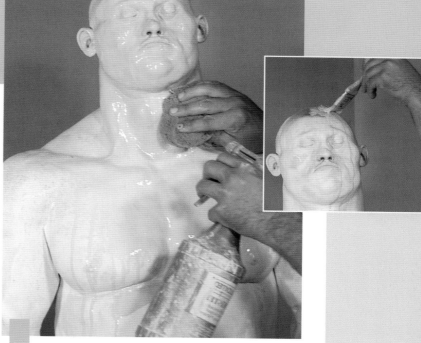

20 To cover the entire figure, a thin base coat of paint (basic flesh) is sprayed on.

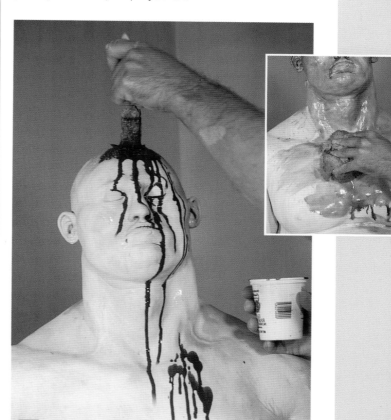

21 To establish a surface that mimics human flesh, successive washes of different colored paints and patinas are sponged and sprayed on.

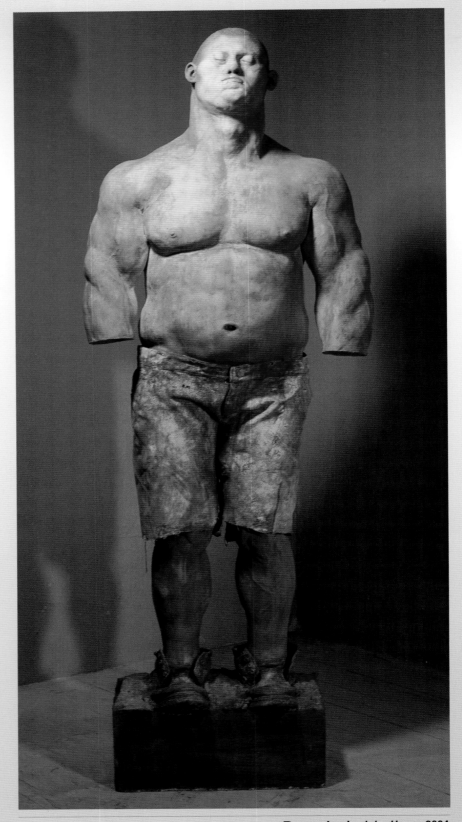

Doug Jeck, *John Henry*, 2004
Coil-built stoneware, concrete, fabric, paint, copper patina
73 x 30 x 18 in. (1.9 m x 76.2 x 45.7 cm)

PHOTO BY REBECCAH KARDONG

GALLERY
OF INVITED ARTISTS

Tim Roda, *Untitled #27, Superhero Complex*, 2003
21¹/₂ x 29¹/₂ in. (54.6 x 74.9 cm)
Earthenware, coil-built slip mixed with plaster, hair,
twist ties, and insects; unfired
PHOTO BY ALLISON RODA

John Byrd, *Untitled: Anatomical Squirrel*, 2003
13 x 21 x 10 in. (33 x 53.3 x 25.4 cm)
Hand-built porcelain; electric fired, bisque cone 5; glaze
cone 05; taxidermy embedded in cast resin
PHOTO BY KEVIN P. DUFFY

**Rebeccah
Kardong**, *Sucker*,
2004
34 x 18 x 24 in.
(86.4 x 45.7 x 61 cm)
Coil-built stoneware;
electric fired, cone 2
PHOTO BY ARTIST

Antonio Pazzi,
Baseball, 1999
54 x 120 x 48 in. (1.4 x 3 x 1.2 m)
Coil-built and slab-built clay,
clothing, slip; gas fired,
cone 04; underglaze
PHOTOS BY ARTIST

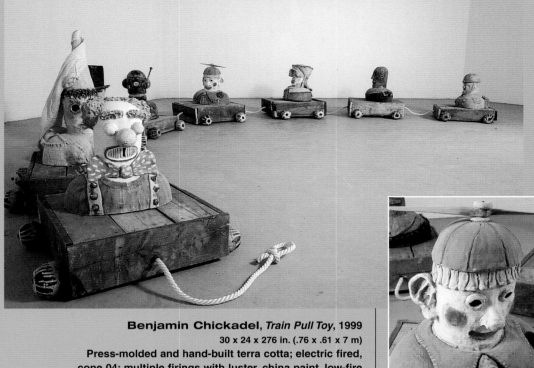

Benjamin Chickadel, *Train Pull Toy*, 1999
30 x 24 x 276 in. (.76 x .61 x 7 m)
Press-molded and hand-built terra cotta; electric fired,
cone 04; multiple firings with luster, china paint, low-fire
glazes, and slips; wood, nylon rope
PHOTOS BY ARTIST

John Byrd, *Untitled (Hunting Dog)*, 2003
17 x 33 x 9 in. (43.2 x 83.8 x 22.9 cm)
Hand-built porcelain; electric fired, bisque cone 3; glaze cone 05; acrylic
paint, dry pigment, taxidermy head embedded in cast resin
PHOTO BY ARTIST

Antonio Pazzi, *Gods Speed*, 2000
36 x 36 x 48 in. (.91 x .91 x 1.2 m)
Coil-built clay, clothing, slip; gas fired,
cone 04; glaze, underglaze
PHOTO BY ARTIST

Doug Jeck

Lauren Grossman,
Sieve, 2001
25 x 11 x 10 in.
(63.5 x 27.9 x 25.4 cm)
Perforated slip-cast
porcelain; electric
fired, cone 6; cast
iron, copper pipe,
rubber squeeze
bulb, liquid

PHOTOS BY
MASZO EVERETT

Doug Jeck has been exhibiting his clay sculpture in solo and group shows for more than 15 years in galleries on both the East and West Coasts, including the Smithsonian Renwick Gallery of the National Museum of American Art in Washington, D.C., and the 55th Scripps Annual at Scripps College in Claremont, California. He received his BFA at the Appalachian Center for Arts and Crafts in Smithville, Tennessee, in 1986 and his MFA at the School of the Art Institute of Chicago in 1989. He currently teaches ceramics at the University of Washington in Seattle.

Mr. Jeck also makes presentations as a lecturer and visiting artist to numerous institutions, including the Rhode Island School of Design in Providence, Rhode Island, and SOFA Chicago (2001). He has also performed the duties of exhibition juror, panelist, and essayist in various academic venues. His awards include the Georgette Koopman Endowed Chair in the Visual Arts at the University of Hartford, Connecticut, and several Virginia A. Groot Foundation grants. Mr. Jeck's work resides in many public and private collections, including the Los Angeles County Museum and the International Museum of Ceramic Art in Alfred, New York.

Justin Novak
THE DISFIGURINE

I WAS BLESSED WITH THE GOOD FORTUNE OF SPENDING MY

adolescent years in the magnificent city of Rome. To say the experience was

formative is indeed an understatement, as there is no part of me that can't

be traced back to its influence, from my aesthetic preferences to my

philosophy of life. The Eternal City is of course brimming with much of the

most astounding art and architecture created over the last 2,500 years, but

as one walks the streets of the city, the most prominent and ambitious

works, by far, are those of the baroque period. The pope and the aristocracy

of the 16th century spared no expense.

Justin Novak,
March of Progress,
1998
14 x 19 x 10 in.
(35.6 x 48.3 x 25.4 cm)
Raku-fired ceramic

PHOTO BY ARTIST

Justin Novak,
Disfigurine
(Competition), 2001
15 x 15 x 15 in.
(38.1 x 38.1 x 38.1 cm)
Raku-fired ceramic
PHOTO BY ARTIST

Inside and out, these massive, opulent edifices are encrusted with gorgeous florid ornamentation. And woven through this adornment are the most masterfully executed larger-than-life figures, in vivid dramatizations of pagan and Catholic narratives. What made such a deep impression on me as a boy just coming of age was their incredibly fluid syntheses of beauty, desire, morality, and power. And that, unlike most decoration we see today, much of that gorgeous ornamentation was there to beautify dark, tragic, and painful stories.

Though baroque painting, such as the work of Caravaggio, had an influence on my decade-long career in New York as a freelance illustrator, it wasn't until I was well into my second career as a ceramist that this inspiration came to full bloom. As I became increasingly drawn to the seductive qualities of clay and the exciting possibilities the medium offered in creating narrative objects, my attention turned once again to the baroque and the more domesticated rococo period into which it evolved. I found that many of the dynamics so familiar to me in monuments of

JUSTIN NOVAK

Justin Novak,
*Apology (for a
Killing) #2,* 2002
**15 x 15 x 10 in.
(38.1 x 38.1 x 25.4 cm)
Raku-fired ceramic**
PHOTO BY ARTIST

marble and bronze were also quite evident in their not-so-distant little cousin, the porcelain figurine.

I'm utterly captivated by the golden era of European porcelain, in late baroque and rococo times, for that period of history certainly represents the height of the figurine, in both craftsmanship and status. I adore, and use, many of the aesthetic conventions of these figurines of old. My pieces have certainly adopted their lyrical and fluid movement, and I purposefully work in a similarly dainty size. I also strive to attain the soft and luscious surface of those antique porcelains, and I borrow liberally from the overly elaborate ornamentation that often encircled them.

The series most central to my work in clay, *Disfigurines*, features figures that are in some way injured or disfigured, and these pieces are certainly influenced by the

> ## Any process of creation is itself full of suggestion.

images of martyrdom that surrounded me in Rome. The title isn't only a play on words (combining the word "disfigure" with the word "figurine"); it also suggests a departure from the traditional object. The figurine, historically, has a long tradition of portraying a perfect world, a dream world, a sentimental and nostalgic or just-plain-cute world. My wounded disfigurines defy those expectations, presenting instead a realm where all is not picture-perfect.

An increasing use of ornament has become as central to the work as the narratives that are suggested by the fig-

ures. The rather lyrical decorative flourishes with which the figures are supported and surrounded (and occasionally even branded) stand in sharp contrast to the evidence of violence. I am fascinated by work that manages to simultaneously seduce and repulse its viewer, and the immediacy and the nuances of the process that I use help me ride that fine line.

Techniques

The methods I employ in building my figurines are rather simple ones. Most of the difficulty lies in the development of a sensitivity to the nuances of the drying process and in learning how to stall that process, when necessary, by misting the work lightly with a spray bottle and selectively wrapping parts of it in plastic. In most cases my figurines are constructed by pinching a rough form out of wet clay, and I gradually refine the surface as the material firms. The first step in this process is invariably to create a maquette, a very small and rough study of the piece, to establish the figure's proportion and gesture. This maquette might be just $1/10$ the size of the piece I envision (often, in my case, a mere 2 inches [5 cm] tall). One of the reasons that the maquette has such a long history of service to the sculptor is that it enables you to perceive the overall composition of your intended piece without the distraction of details. This is particularly valuable in the case of figurative work, in which the effort to achieve anatomical accuracy can eclipse the pursuit of dynamic formal composition.

The emotionally and symbolically charged use of gesture is central to the success of classic figurines, and my process of building up the forms with very wet clay enables me to capture the spontaneity and nuance that are needed. This process, however, couldn't be further from the exact methods of mass production used to create those historical figurines, and the immediacy of my process enables me to make decisions, in the moment, that exaggerate or distort the figure in numerous ways. Though I don't often employ distortion to an extreme, I do find that the liberties I take in the articulation of anatomy often contribute to the emotional impact of the work.

110

Though my inspiration is from the tradition of European porcelain, I have only recently begun working in porcelain itself. Much of my work is raku fired ceramic, a time-honored low-fire technique adopted from Japan that has evolved into its own distinctly American one. The distressed, crackled surface that the process yields seemed to lend itself naturally to the suffering portrayed in my figures. The stress and damage to which the pieces were subjected in some way echoed their painful predicament.

The newest works presented here, made of white stoneware or porcelain itself, are referring more directly to the historical figurines that inspired them. Working with very soft, elastic porcelain is a novel (and exceedingly difficult) experience for me. The challenges of keeping the clay moist and workable are amplified, as the highly refined porcelain is most unforgiving. It doesn't remain pliable for long, and it's fond of cracking with the slightest unevenness in wall thickness or moisture level, but I find the results to be most gratifying. I'm excited and intrigued by the thought of working with a material similar to that of late-18th- and early-19th-century figurine production. In this manner I'm working within a specific tradition even as I seek to evolve and subvert it. In the most recent of the disfigurines, glossy commercial glazes on the smooth, highly refined porcelain deliver a surface that is strikingly different from a crackled raku effect, with its antiqued patina. Little remains of the coarseness and character of those earlier surfaces as I embrace an aesthetic that has a closer relationship to the commercial figurine of this era. And though I have a strong attraction to the crackled glaze, I believe the pristine surface perhaps invites a more contemporary interpretation.

I share this process in the hope that you'll benefit from the technique being illustrated, but in doing so, I'd like to emphasize that the process and content of this body of work are not the result of the pursuit of a clear conception, but rather a gradual evolution. My process has been one of allowing intuition to lead, but also of pausing frequently to reflect on the developing work and to shift, redirect, and exploit those intuitive impulses so that they might resonate

Justin Novak,
Canopied Figure (#1), **2000**
21 x 6 x 4 in.
(53.3 x 15.2 x 10.2 cm)
Raku-fired ceramic
PHOTO BY ARTIST
COURTESY NANCY MARGOLIS GALLERY

culturally. Process and content have thus evolved together, hand in hand, throughout the many transformations the work has undergone—from specific to less explicit narratives, from rough-textured surfaces to smoother, more sensual ones, from classic but simple hourglass bases to highly ornate pedestals. In this manner, the resulting work, at its best, possesses both intelligence and raw intensity.

Any process of creation is itself full of suggestion; if accompanied by attentiveness to the history and the future possibilities of the medium, it can open up wonderful new territories.

Justin Novak,
Lap of Luxury, **2000**
8 x 20 x 9 in. (20.3 x 50.8 x 22.9 cm)
Raku-fired ceramic
PHOTO BY ARTIST
COURTESY NANCY MARGOLIS GALLERY

TECHNIQUE: PINCH

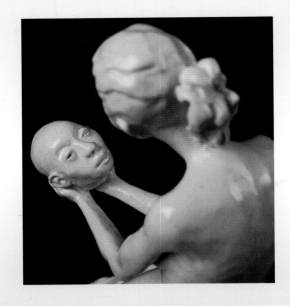

 1 For further reference, the maquette is often accompanied by a drawing to actual scale.

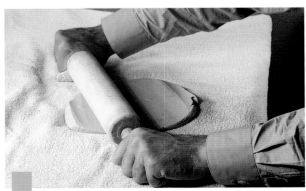

2 The construction of the piece begins with rolling slabs to a thickness of about $^3/_8$ inch (.95 cm).

3 Cutting the shape of one of the slabs to conform to the footprint of the piece and pinching up the form from the edges with other fragments of similar slabs, or with handfuls of clay taken straight from the bucket. These additions are blended or kneaded into the interior surface as well as the exterior of the developing shell, thus creating the strongest possible bond.

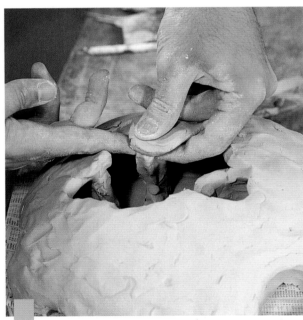

4 The form is built up evenly from the base, and, at the same time, strategically placed internal supporting walls are created that will support the weight of the figures to come.

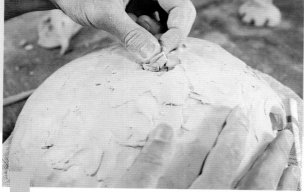

5 Finishing the hollow form by blending a small plug of clay over a supporting interior wall, thus allowing for some pressure as the plug is smoothed into the surface. An inconspicuous pinhole is poked through the side or underside of the shell in order to avoid chambers of trapped air, which can pose a threat during the firing process.

6 At this point I allow the clay to firm up just a bit, to that most desirable stage where it holds its form yet is still somewhat malleable. Before I begin sculpting the figures, I score the pattern of the pedestal's decorative features and add those forms by pressing on thin coils of clay.

7 Scoring the surface at those points where the figure or figures make contact with the base form ...

8 ... then constructing the figurative components, starting with the solid forms of feet and lower legs. Once the knee is formed, I begin again to pinch a hollow form for the thighs. Any part of the body 1 inch (2.5 cm) or more thick is constructed as a hollow section.

9 As the developing form arrives at a point where the wet clay seems to be unable to support its weight, I bolster it with a generous-sized post of clay. This temporary buttress will need to be cut away, but not until the material has firmed up quite a bit and is strong enough to fully support itself.

10 I continue pinching the form hollow, joining the two thighs at the groin as I transition to the torso. By gently pushing out the clay wall as the form emerges, I can start articulating separate volumes of the body, such as the abdomen, rib cage, and breast.

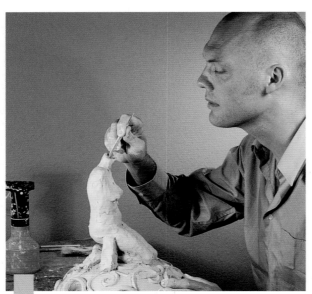

11 Momentarily ignoring the arms, I close off the form at the shoulders and pinch to the narrow cylinder of the neck. Depending on its thickness, sometimes I choose to render the neck solid, remembering to poke a small hole in the head to avoid an enclosed air chamber.

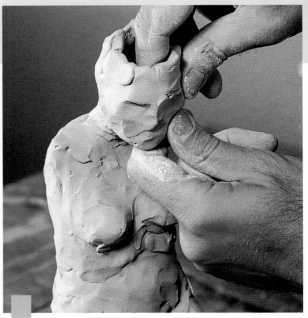

12 The head is pinched hollow, roughing in skeletal structures such as cranium, jawline, cheekbones, and brow.

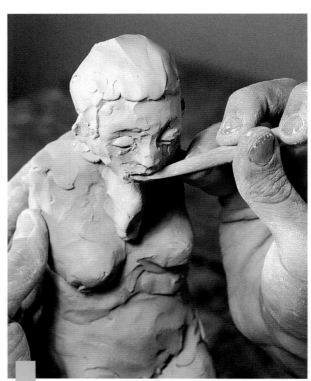

13 The eyelids, nose, ears, and lips are rendered with the help of a fine flat wooden tool once the form is closed at the top, at which point I once again allow the piece to firm up.

14 This time I take care to cover areas that are already firm and in danger of drying out excessively, particularly the shoulder area, to which I'll be adding more clay.

16 The arms are formed in position, taking advantage of the wet clay to capture a fluid gesture that would be much more difficult to achieve with leather-hard assembly.

15 Returning to the piece after the material has had some time to firm, I pinch out the arms from the shoulder area after the surface being joined has been moistened and scored.

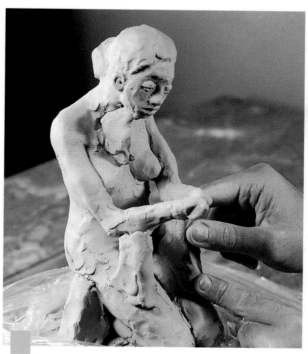

17 Once more, solid supports are employed whenever the force of gravity prohibits progress.

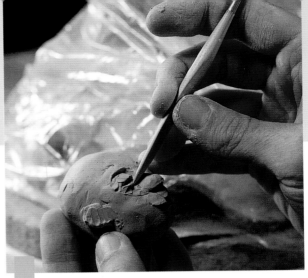

20 Roughing in the details

18 The hands are created initially as very loose gestural forms.

21 The added weight of a disembodied head will be placed in the hands, so a strong pillar must be added for support before tackling the delicate job of refining the details in the hands.

19 The hands are articulated with fine wood tools or a very small wire loop tool.

22 After the last anatomical details or decorative flourishes are added, the entire piece is allowed to firm up to the point where the surface is resistant to impressions of the hand but still soft enough to whittle down, even with a blunt tool.

23 Fine metal loops and their pointed wood ends are used for meticulous detail.

24 As the clay continues to firm, I take the precaution of plastic-wrapping thinner limbs that might be prone to cracking if they dry much faster than the rest of the body. Even at relatively advanced stages of the drying process, the finest of details can still be executed crisply with a fresh, razor-sharp craft knife.

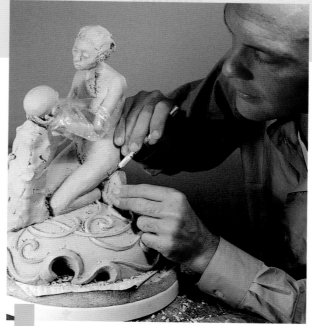

25 As the material reaches the leather-hard state (very firm but still damp), the temporary posts that served to buttress the form can be removed. Some might have fused to the figure in spots, requiring the use of the craft knife to cut them away.

26 At times the figure so tenuously supports its own weight that these posts must be replaced with smaller ones, to be left in place till the very end (and removed only when the piece is safely in the kiln).

27 Finally, the elimination of unwanted surface texture is achieved with a moistened kitchen scrubber in the case of broader areas, followed with refinement by hand-smoothing the clay.

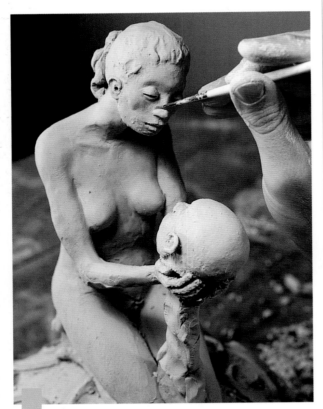

28 Areas featuring fine detail can be smoothed with a moist, soft brush, allowing for an articulation of form that is both soft and sharply defined.

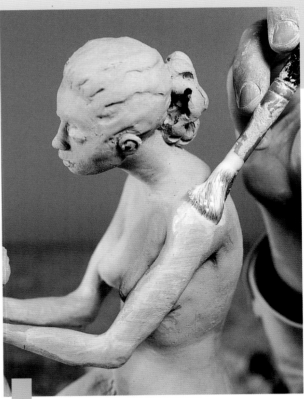

29 Once the piece is well into the drying process, which must be slow and thorough before firing, underglazes are brushed on.

30 After lightly sponging the surface to remove dust, a thin coat of glaze is applied by brush to the bisque-fired piece.

RAKU CLEAR	
Gerstley borate	80
Nepheline syenite	20
Total	**100**

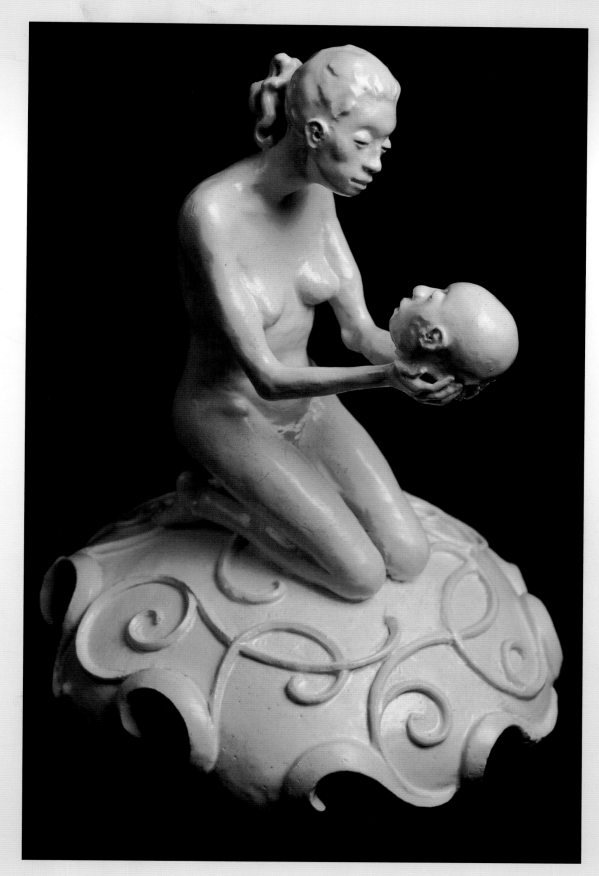

Justin Novak
Untitled, 2004
12 x 9 x 9 in.
(30.5 x 22.9 x 22.9 cm)
PHOTO BY AMJAD
SALEH FAUR

GALLERY
OF INVITED ARTISTS

Cynthia Consentino, *Rabbit Girl*, 2003
30 1/4 x 20 x 17 1/4 in. (76.8 x 50.8 x 43.8 cm)
Coil- and slab-built earthenware; electric
fired, cone 05; terra sigillata, oils, cold wax

PHOTO BY JOHN POLAK

Cynthia Consentino, *Flower Girl,* 2004
35 1/2 x 22 x 39 in. (90.2 x 55.9 x 99.1 cm)
Coil- and slab-built earthenware; electric fired,
cone 05; oil paint over terra sigillata, cold wax

PHOTOS BY ARTIST

Georges Jeanclos, *Urne,* 1979–1980
13 x 17 x 15 in. (33 x 43.2 x 38.1 cm)
Fired terra cotta

PHOTO BY ANTHONY CUÑHA. COURTESY OF FRANK LLOYD
GALLERY AND THE ESTATE OF GEORGES JEANCLOS

Cynthia Consentino, *Tom Boy,* 2004
24 x 14 x 8 1/2 in. (61 x 35.6 x 21.6 cm)
Coil- and solid-built earthenware; electric
fired, cone 04; underglaze, glaze

PHOTO BY ARTIST

Meredith Younger, *Untitled*, 2004
17 x 14 x 10 in. (43.2 x 35.6 x 25.4 cm)
Coil-built stoneware; fired in
oxidation, cone 2
PHOTO BY ARTIST

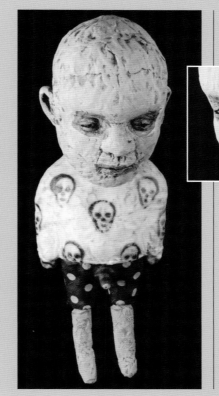

Tom Bartel,
Death and Life Figure, 2003
18 x 8 x 8 in. (45.7 x 20.3 x 20.3 cm)
Coil-built red stoneware;
electric multi-fired, cone 02;
vitreous engobe, black copper
oxide, wire; stenciled, stamped
PHOTOS BY JOE IMEL

Meredith Younger,
Homeless Child, 2003
26 x 10 x 9 in. (66 x 25.4 x 22.9 cm)
Coil-built stoneware; fired in
oxidation, cone 2
PHOTOS BY ARTIST

Georges Jeanclos,
Grande Barque, 1991
66 x 13 x 16¾ in. (1.7 x .33 x .43 m)
Fired terra cotta

PHOTO BY ANTHONY CUÑHA. COURTESY OF
FRANK LLOYD GALLERY AND THE ESTATE OF
GEORGES JEANCLOS

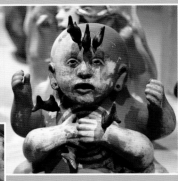

Fish Dards
21 x 16 x 12 in. (53.3 x 40.6 x 30.5 cm)
**Press-molded and hand-built
low-fire clay; terra sigilatta, cone 1**

PHOTOS BY DOUGLAS HERREN

Kukuli Velarde, *Isichapuitu Series/Installation*, 2001
Each, 23 x 12 x 10 in. (58.4 x 30.5 x 25.4 cm)
Press-molded and hand-built low-fire clay; glazes, enamels, oil, acrylic

PHOTO BY ARTIST

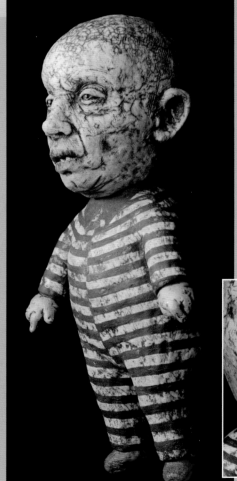

Tom Bartel, *Figure from Earth*, 2002
20 x 10 x 10 in. (50.8 x 25.4 x 25.4 cm)
**Coil-built red stoneware; electric
multi-fired, cone 02; vitreous engobe,
black copper oxide**

PHOTOS BY JOE IMEL

Justin Novak

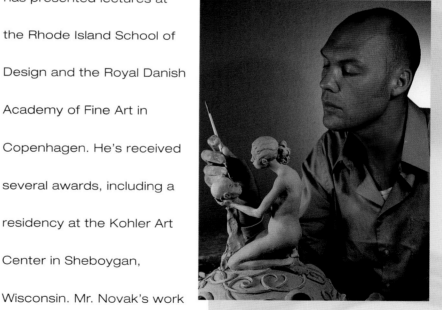

Justin Novak lives in Eugene, Oregon, where he teaches ceramics at the University of Oregon. He received his BFA from the Pratt Institute in New York in 1983 and an MFA from the State University of New York at New Paltz in 1996. His work is exhibited in both group and solo shows in the United States and Europe, including the John Elder Gallery and Greenwich House Pottery in New York City and the Walbrzych Muzeum in Walbrzych, Poland. As a visiting artist, Mr. Novak has presented lectures at the Rhode Island School of Design and the Royal Danish Academy of Fine Art in Copenhagen. He's received several awards, including a residency at the Kohler Art Center in Sheboygan, Wisconsin. Mr. Novak's work has been reviewed and featured in various print venues and resides in both public and private collections.

Tom Bartel,
Figure in Diaper and Glasses, 2003
20 x 8 x 10 in. (50.8 x 20.3 x 25.4 cm)
Coil-built red stoneware; electric multi-fired, cone 02; vitreous engobe, black copper oxide
PHOTO BY JOE IMEL

Nan Smith
THROUGH THE EYE

VISUAL ART PRACTICE IS A SOLITARY ENDEAVOR WHEREIN

the art mirrors those things the artist values. Introspective by nature, I'm compelled by the mysteries of life, to ask questions about why we're here. William Blake's lines, "To See A World in a Grain of Sand, / And a Heaven in a Wild Flower," reflect my search for a higher level of awareness.

Nan Smith, *Visionary*, 1995
Installation: 108 x 300 x 420 in. (2.7 x 7.6 x 10.6 m)
Press-molded, assembled, and sculpturally detailed earthenware; electric fired, cone 03; airbrushed underglaze, textural and transparent matte glazes, acrylic bisque stains, gypsum cement, stainless steel, wood
PHOTO BY ALLEN CHEUVRONT

Nan Smith, *Visionary*
(detail), 1995

PHOTO BY ALLEN CHEUVRONT

Nan Smith,
Beyond Illusions,
2001
Installation:
92 x 72 x 192 in.
(2.3 x 1.8 x 4.9 m)
Press-molded,
assembled, and
sculpturally detailed
earthenware;
electric fired, cone
03; airbrushed
underglaze, glaze,
textural and
matte glazes,
bisque stains,
gypsum cement,
water jet-cut
stainless steel,
wood, backlit
photograph
PHOTO BY DAVID RAMSEY

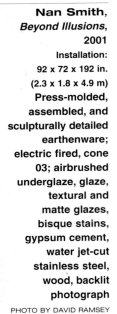

Expression and gesture indicate moments of contemplation.

Making sculpture that speaks about the inner state of consciousness is important to me. The human image has always fascinated me, and it's through figure sculpture that I reach out to touch my world. My ideas often appear as an early morning thought where, in my mind's eye, I glimpse a figure moving within an ethereal space. In a sculpture, whether I'm working with a single female figure or a grouping, the expression and gesture indicate moments of contemplation. I use the spatial design of the tableau to project this stillness, outwardly. This unity of the inner and outer worlds reflects my belief in the connectedness of life.

Once I visualize an idea, the real work begins. I develop the initial concept by reading and looking at related imagery. Since I don't work in series, I do numerous designs and drawings and often build parts more than once to become skillful with a new form. I carefully select my models, often choosing one for her face, another for her hands, and still another for her body. I usually photograph each young woman and use this information for visual and anatomical reference.

I choose to present the female form as a young adult, an age that reflects potential and the ability for self-evolution, and also as a symbol of the intuitive self. Each sculpture is an idealized composite that personifies innocence. I envisioned *White Mood* as a woman in repose gesturing as though in the midst of a thought. I chose a bust format because I wanted to reflect her sensitivity through the tilt of her head and the movement of her hand. A favorite book of vintage Hollywood portraits revealed a picture of Garbo that provided the elegant gesture I was searching for. I wanted to place the bust and hand within a defined space in such a way that the upper body would be implied. Through slip-dipped remnants of lace surrounding the clay pedestal, I hoped to create elegance and offer a timeless quality. The pedestal is a platform on which the figure is set intimately, like a jewel. The monochromatic color scheme of white on white recalls statuary, but the varied surfaces of the white-toned glazes indicate subtle material differences. I feel that the restrained color and textural variety reinforce the idealism and allow the viewer to enter the world I am setting forth.

Process

The materials and methods I use to make molds are as varied as the forms I choose to cast. These molds are tools for me, and I often experiment with new materials in order to develop more effective techniques. When I take a cast from a life model, I try to work directly with plaster, but if it requires more than a two-piece mold or has a complex motion, I use other materials. The many planes of a gesturing hand are a challenge if you cast from life, because they require individual mold sections. I use flexible molds (the alginate and rubber ones) to simplify the number of sections needed for such a complex and heavily undercut form. The mold-making process shown here has five stages, from a negative alginate casting to a positive plaster model to a rubber mold with a cradling plaster mother mold to, finally, the press-molded clay. I also cast alginate to make plaster models of fine lace, from which I also make a rubber press mold. Similarly, the draped fabric of a skirt or blouse is first created in plaster before rubber molds are made. When building my life-size figures, I press-mold the body in sections and assemble parts: the head, torso, arms, hands, and lower body. In addition to casting, I do a lot of freehand modeling to create a continuous form, remove seam lines, and sculpt details like hair and eyebrows. The press-

molded element can be altered each time I use it, allowing me to use the mold for more than one sculpture with a variety of results.

The face, torso, and hand casts for *White Mood* were taken from three different women. The life casts for the head and torso were made with U.S. Gypsum's #1 molding plaster because it has an extended work time and is easy to form into a "slush casting." I'm careful to keep the mold thin (1 to 2 inches [2.5 to 5 cm]) so that as it cures it doesn't get too hot for the skin. The life casting for the sculpture's hand was taken by submerging the model's hand within alginate, an algae-based, nontoxic casting material used by dentists. Once the model's hand is removed, I pour plaster into this mold to create a plaster duplicate. A rubber mold is then taken from the plaster form. In the past I've used latex rubber, but more recently I've started using a two-part flexible polyurethane rubber. This molding material can be applied by brush in three or four $\frac{1}{4}$-inch (6 mm) layers, whereas a latex mold requires 15 very thin coats. Using polyurethane is faster and, unlike latex, it doesn't shrink. A supporting plaster

Nan Smith,
Guardian, **1997**
Installation: 92 x 138 x 92 in. (2.3 x 3.5 x 2.3 m) Press-molded, assembled, and sculpturally detailed earthenware; electric fired, cone 03; airbrushed underglaze, textural and matte glazes, stainless steel, aluminum, wood
PHOTO BY ALLEN CHEUVRONT

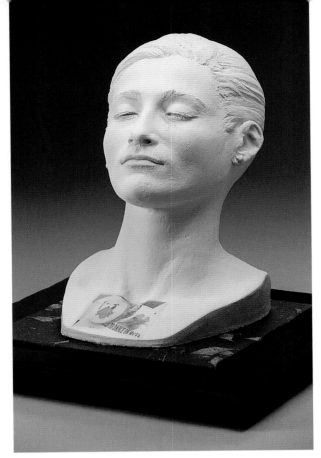

Nan Smith,
Secret, 2004
15 x 14 x 12 in.
(38.1 x 35.6 x 30.5 cm)
Press-molded,
assembled, and
detailed earthen-
ware; electric fired,
cone 03; airbrushed
underglaze, matte
glaze, laser decals,
cone 08

PHOTO BY ALLEN
CHEUVRONT

Nan Smith,
Clarity, 2002
27 1/2 x 23 1/2 x 20 in.
(69.9 x 59.7 x 50.8 cm)
Press-molded,
assembled, and
detailed earthen-
ware; electric fired,
cone 03; airbrushed
transparent matte
and textural glazes,
bisque stains

PHOTO BY ALLEN
CHEUVRONT

mold is cast over each rubber section so that it can be used as a press mold. Once the molds are dry and cured, I press plastic clay slabs into the plaster and the rubber molds. While the clay is still in the mold, I compress the surface with a rubber rib, then create a stable structure on the inside by inserting clay "studs" within the walls and clay flanges at the joints. Only then can I work on the piece's exterior.

In an effort to express an idealist aesthetic, I maintain the realism of the casting by carefully removing any imperfections before assembling the parts. Small lines at the seam edges and fissures in the chest, which were caused when the model breathed during the casting process, are smoothed and retextured. I assemble the front and back sections of the torso and the head, and when each is leather-hard I carefully cut and fit the neck onto its shoulders. During this careful fitting process I make adjustments to the basic casting to create the tilt and turn of the head. I unify the form by continuing to sculpt the figure once it's assembled.

I'm careful to slowly dry each section by wrapping it in heavy bath towels to blot the moisture, replacing damp towels with dry ones until the clay's color changes and it becomes partially bone-dry. Before glazing, I do glaze test tiles and then test surface patterns on larger tiles. I fire in electric kilns and pro-gram their controllers to heat and slowly cool the fir-ings. I program a cool-down cycle to obtain more even cooling and to prevent bottom cracking.

Space and Emptiness

Spatial design is a personal love. Whether arrang-ing small objects on a shelf or planting a flower gar-den, I delight in relating things and working with space. Learning Chinese calligraphy, ikebana, and the Japanese tea ceremony helped develop my acute sensitivity to space and its organization. Emptiness in my work is a contrast to the detailed imagery; what is shown calls into question what is not visible. I have always seen negative space as vital, for it is this sense of air that transports and opens a composition. The scale of the elements and how they exist in space are primary considerations in my sculpture.

Art functions on many levels: the physical, emotional, intellectual, and spiritual. I find that placing the figure in context or working with an installation orientation, as the sculptor and architect Bernini did, has infinite possibility. As a sculptor my goal is to contribute to the recognition that spiritual evolution is a human possibility. I believe that one can meet the challenge of creating large-scale ceramic sculpture in innovative ways and with an attitude of play. A wealth of information about techniques is available through formal programs, publications, and workshops. These can be the beginning, but the most important accomplishments tend to happen in the silence of what one friend calls the "deep studio."

Nan Smith,
A Reliquary, 2004.
16 x 16 ⅛ x 21 in.
(40.6 x 40.7 x 53.3 cm).
Press-molded, assembled, and detailed earthenware; slab and lace-draped tile; electric fired, cone 03; airbrushed, matte white glaze, laser decals, cone 08.
PHOTO BY ALLEN CHEUVRONT

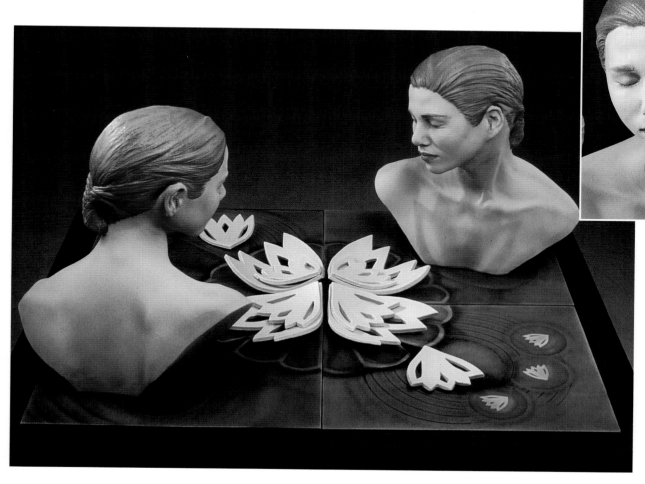

Nan Smith,
Oneness, 1999
54 ¾ x 34 ½ x 40 ¼ in.
(1.4 x .988 x 1 m)
Press-molded, assembled, and detailed earthenware tiles; slab-constructed earthenware slump molds; electric fired, cone 03; airbrushed textural and matte glazes, and bisque stains
PHOTO BY
ALLEN CHEUVRONT

TECHNIQUE:
CASTING
+ MOLDS

Nan Smith,
White Mood,
2004

PHOTO BY
ALLAN CHEUVRONT

2 The area around the nose and nostrils is carefully built up. No straws are placed into the nose because they would distort the shape of the nostrils. The plaster is applied, no more than 2 inches (5 cm) thick, in two thin coats and a thicker final coat. I keep the layer to this thickness so that the curing plaster doesn't create too much heat on the skin.

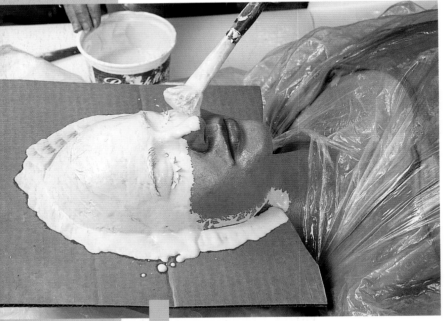

1 The first thin coat of plaster is carefully brushed onto the model's face. Brushing avoids air bubbles and allows the plaster to pick up small details. All areas of the skin and hair, including eyelashes and brows, were first coated with petroleum jelly. The custom-fit piece of cardboard acts as a separating plane during the casting.

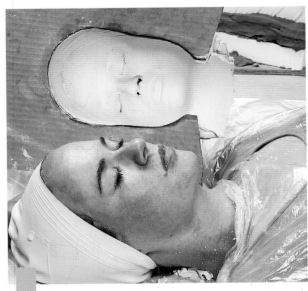

3 After approximately 30 minutes, the hardened plaster mold is removed from the face. I use a blow dryer to help speed the set time of the plaster.

4 The model's hand is inserted into ungelled alginate held in a container that's proportionate in size and shape to that of the posed hand. It will take 7–8 minutes for the material to set.

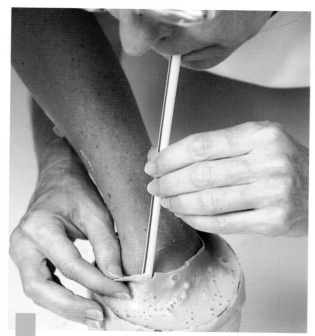

5 A straw is used to blow air into the casting before the model carefully pulls free.

6 Plaster is mixed immediately and poured into the alginate mold. I tap the table so that all air bubbles rise to the surface of the casting.

7 To avoid breaking any extended fingers, I wait a full day before removing the alginate from the plaster casting.

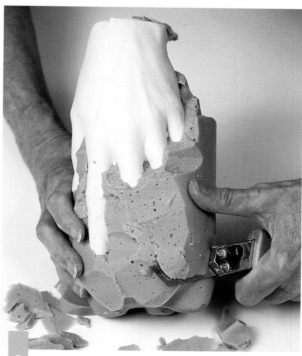

8 The mold is destroyed when it's cut away from the plaster cast. If the casting has undercuts, the alginate mold can be used only once.

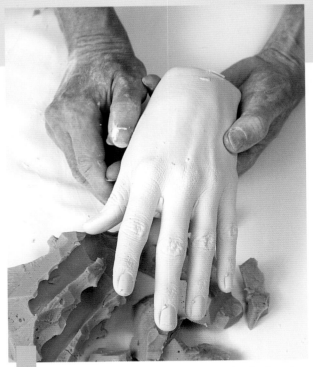

9 The resulting plaster cast is highly detailed and requires only minimal cleanup before use as the model for a rubber mold.

11 Building the separating plane of a two-piece mold. In order to avoid undercuts in the mold, a bisecting section line was first drawn all around the hand at the height of its outermost convex curves. Wads of soft clay support the hand so that it's level to the tabletop. More clay is used to build the rest of the mold's bottom half.

12 The clay wall will retain the liquid rubber as it's brushed on. Notice that the bisecting plane, carefully smoothed with a rib, undulates along the pencilled section line. Convex "keys" will align the mold's two halves.

10 Two coats of mold soap are painted onto the plaster model to seal it. Once the soap is fully dry, a resist agent is sprayed onto both the clay and the model.

13 The mold rubbers, resin, and catalyst are mixed, in a 1:1 ratio by weight or volume, for about 2 minutes with a wooden tongue depressor. I wear vinyl gloves to protect my hands.

14 Three coats of the rubber mixture are applied with a paintbrush within a 3- to 4-hour period. The clay should be moist or leather-hard. A thickener called cabosil is added to the third and final coat of rubber, and small pieces of a woven polyester fabric are inlaid into the edge (to reinforce it) as the third coat is applied; each piece is thoroughly saturated.

15 The thickness of the rubber mold is checked by cutting a notch into the clay wall and lifting the edge, which should have an average thickness of 3/4 to 1 inch (1.9 to 2.5 cm). The polyurethane rubber is allowed to cure for 24 hours.

16 Paste wax, which will act as a resist agent, is applied to the rubber with a sponge before making the plaster mother, or slush, mold.

17 The initial coat of plaster, called the "gel coat," is flicked onto the rubber mold with the fingers. It sounds like rain hitting a surface. The impact limits any air bubbles that might form on the surface of the cast.

20 Wooden wedges and a mallet are used to tap at the section line. Tapping at three different places along the line should open the mold.

18 The plaster mother mold is built up. On smaller molds the wall thickness of the plaster should be no less than 1^1/$_2$ inches (3.8 cm). After the plaster has cured and the clay wall is removed, the second half of the rubber mold and plaster mother mold will be cast.

21 The rubber mold easily peels away from the plaster model. The polyurethane mold will be stored within its mother mold in a cool, dry place, away from ultraviolet light.

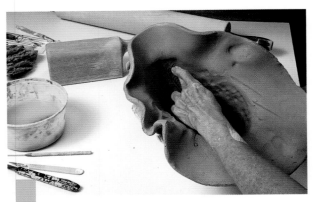

19 The section line created by the rubber layer is revealed in the plaster by sanding it with a Surform tool.

22 The surface of a plastic clay slab is smoothed, using a rib and water, prior to press molding it into the head mold. It's important to bend the clay as you extend it into the mold. I add extra clay to the low, concave areas.

23 Adding a coil to the perimeter of the clay wall while still wet. This flange will be used later to join other sections to this one.

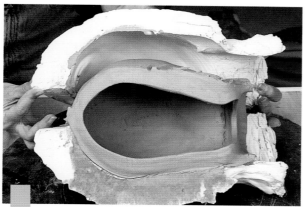

24 When the clay is leather-hard, it's removed from the molds. The back of the head is cast in two pieces, then any mars and imperfections are removed from each piece.

25 Adding clay "studs" to the inside of the torso form gives added support to the sculpture during the building and firing processes.

26 Water is brushed onto clay flanges and they're scored until they look like wet concrete. I use a Chinese scoring tool, which has many sharp prongs, to quickly score the clay. I don't add slip, but allow the water and abraded clay to produce a "self-slip" that I use to bond the sections.

27 By balancing the front and back halves of the clay torso against each other, I make the form stand upright. The flanges are worked together in the interior to secure the joint.

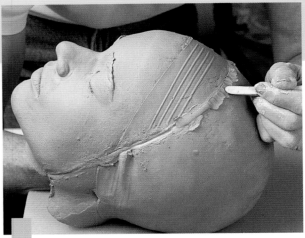

28 The bottom slab has a hole cut into it (so that air can escape) before it can be joined to the torso. Slabs of clay are added to the shoulders and the bottom of the form to enclose it. After this is completed, all outer joints are carefully detailed.

30 The face and back of the head are carefully joined. The clay flanges are worked together on the inside of the form to create a continuous bond.

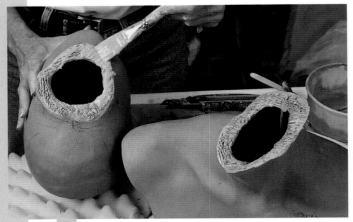

29 The head and neck flanges are scored before the head is attached to the torso.

31 The ears are formed by pressing clay into a rubber mold then further detailed using the plaster life casting as a visual reference.

NAN SMITH'S SCULPTURE CLAY RECIPE

Fire to cone 03–01

Talc	8.7
OM-4 ball clay (can substitute C&C)	13.9
AP Green fire clay	15.6
Goldart clay	20.9
Ocmulgee clay (can substitute Lizella)	6.1
Fine silica sand, 80–90 mesh (Feldspar Corp.)	17.4
Fine grog (Christy Minerals STKO-2205)	17.4
Total	**100**

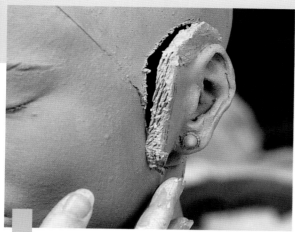

32 The ear is placed into the side of the head. Both ears are aligned and then permanently sculpted into place.

33 A very thin slab of clay is pounded with a wooden mallet. I spray the surface with water and rib it before pressing it into the rubber mold, then smooth the back of the slab after pressing it in. It can be peeled away right after making the impression and used immediately to form a fabriclike surface.

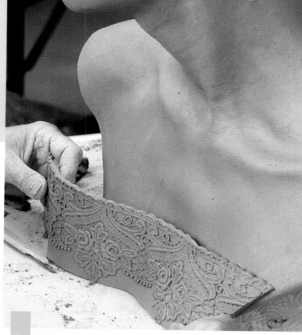

34 The bodice is contoured to the form and then attached.

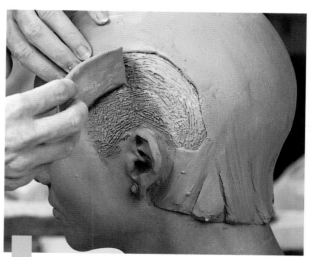

35 A veneer of clay strips laid onto the head lets me create hair with movement and dimension.

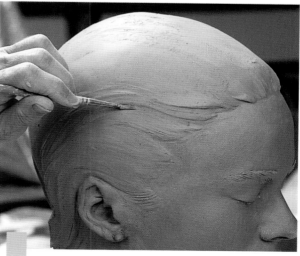

36 The locks of hair are modeled and smoothed using a small paintbrush.

37 The ceramic hand has been press-molded into the two-piece polyurethane rubber mold. Later, the bottom of the hand is cut out, and a slab with a dowel-size hole will be attached to it. A wooden dowel will be used to hold the hand onto the clay pedestal.

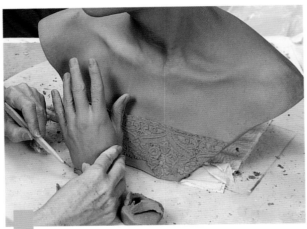

38 Clay is carefully cut away in order to establish the angle at which the hand will stand. The disc shown in photo 37 will be used to close the hollow hand so it can stand upright on a dowel.

39 All of the slabs needed are made on a slab roller in a single day. Foam board templates are traced with a needle tool. The shapes are cut with a craft knife, using a metal ruler as a guide, when the clay becomes leather-hard.

40 The edges are scored and the walls are added to the bottom slab, using a carpenter's square to be sure each side is perpendicular to the bottom. A coil is carefully worked into every inside joint.

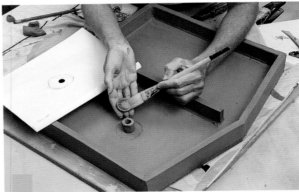

41 A wall is joined to the center of the pedestal to act as a support during firing. The position of the hand is transferred from the foam board template to the inside of the pedestal, where a hole is cut for a hollow clay tube. The tube will be capped at the bottom so it can hold a wooden dowel in place when the pedestal tile is right side up.

42 After flipping the leather-hard pedestal is flipped (using two supporting wooden boards), pieces of lace are saturated in slip made from the base clay recipe. Excess slip is removed by laying the lace onto a smooth tabletop and ribbing it.

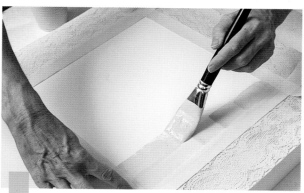

43 The lace is laid onto a thin application of slip. The pedestal will be dried facedown; a cloth towel over it will absorb the moisture slowly and prevent warping.

44 Color and glaze tests are done prior to glazing. An airbrush is used to apply commercial underglaze to the surface of the sculpture.

45 The ceramic bust, hand, and pedestal are airbrushed with a white underglaze. Airbrushing gives a smooth and even coating and doesn't interfere with surface detail. Glaze will be sprayed on when the underglaze is completely dry.

46 The pedestal is coated with two glazes. A rectangle is measured and drawn, and a resist made of masking tape and paper is laid inside it before the first glaze is sprayed.

47 The second glaze, which requires a thicker application, is painted onto the surface with a large paintbrush. Tape keeps the hard edge and resists the second glaze as it's applied.

Nan Smith, *White Mood,* 2004
20¹/₂ x 16¹/₈ x 17¹/₂ in. (52.1 x 41.5 x 44.5 cm)
Underglazed and glazed earthenware, electric fired, cone 03

PHOTO BY ALLAN CHEUVRONT

GALLERY
OF INVITED ARTISTS

Marilyn Lysohir
The Dark Side of Dazzle (Figure and Sink), 1986
6 x 10 x 5 in. (15.2 x 25.4 x 12.7 cm)
Coil-built low-fire talc body; electric fired, gas
fired, cone 05; terra sigillata

PHOTO BY ARTIST

Keith Wallace Smith, *Incarceration*, 1999
27 x 27 x 34 in. (68.6 x 68.6 x 86.4 cm)
Press-molded terra cotta; gas fired, cone 04; engobe
sprayed on green, cone 04; iron bars

PHOTO BY ALLEN CHEUVRONT

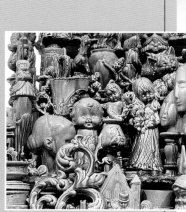

Walter McConnell,
Theory of Everything, 2004
.83 x 6 x 6 ft. (.25 x 1.8 x 1.8 m)
Porcelain cast from commercial
molds; glazed and fused, cone
7; plywood, polystyrene

PHOTO BY ARTIST

Katy Rush, *Sandals*, 2004
7 x 6 x 7 in. (17.8 x 15.2 x 17.8 cm)
Slip-cast porcelain; electric fired, cone 6

PHOTO BY ARTIST

Lisa Marie Barber, *Little City*, 2002
68 x 85 x 93 in. (1.7 x 2.2 x 2.4 m)
Hand-built, coil-built, slab-built, and
pinched recycled clay mixed with sawdust;
gas fired in oxidation, cone 03 or 04;
multi-fired glazes, gas or electric fired in
oxidation between cone 03 and cone 07
PHOTO BY DAVID PACE

Linda Ganstrom, *Patience*, 2004
5 x 14 x 84 in. (.12 x .36 x 2.1 m)
Slab-built stoneware press molded in body-cast molds;
gas fired, bisque cone 04; stained, cone 04

PHOTO BY MITCH WEBER, CTELT, FORT HAYS STATE UNIVERSITY

Renee Wirtz-Audette,
Little Miss Sensitive, 2003
11 x 5 x 5 in. (27.9 x 12.7 x 12.7 cm)
Hand-built porcelain; electric
fired, cone 6; stains and underglaze, cone 6; metal music box

PHOTO BY JOHN KNAUB

Elaina Wendt, *Gift,* **2002**
52 x 32 x 24 in. (1.3 x .81 x .61 m)
Slab-built terra cotta; unfired;
found object, video projection
PHOTO BY ARTIST

Ovidio Giberga, *Seated Male Vessel with*
Organic Binding, **2004**
21 x 16 x 13 in. (53.3 x 40.6 x 33 cm)
Slip-cast earthenware; electric fired; terra sig-
illata, low-fire glaze, china paints, cone 04
PHOTO BY ARTIST

Nan Smith

Nan Smith has taught ceramics at the University of
Florida and maintained her private studio in Gainesville
since 1979. She has also taught at the University of Illinois
and Ohio State University. She holds degrees in ikebana
and Japanese tea ceremony, having completed inde-
pendent studies at the Japan House at the University of
Illinois with Tea Master Shozo Sato.

Ms. Smith has presented workshops on latex mold making
and airbrush for ceramics throughout the United States,
including the 1999 National Council on Education for the
Ceramic Arts Conference. She has been a resident artist
twice at the Watershed Center for Ceramic Arts, and she
recently curated a ceramic installation and a figurative
ceramic sculpture exhibition. She has received individual
artist fellowships from the NEA-funded Southern Arts
Federation and the state of
Florida, plus awards for teaching
excellence from the University
of Florida. Her pieces reside in
many ceramics collections,
including the WOCEK
International Ceramics Collection
in Korea. Her work was featured
at the 2004 SOFA Chicago, and
has been exhibited in such art
venues as the the Contemporary
Art Center in New Orleans,
Louisiana. They have also been
reproduced in numerous ceramics magazines and books,
such as *Clay and Glazes for the Potter* (Krause
Publications, 2000), *The Craft and Art of Clay* (Overlook
Press, 2003), and *500 Figures in Clay* (Lark Books, 2004).

Akio Takamori
THE SURFACE AS CANVAS

WHO DO I SEE WHEN I LOOK AT YOU? HOW DO YOU VIEW ME?

Can we ever look at something without having already formed assumptions? These questions lead me to think about how perception and identity relate and inform each other. I try to articulate these ideas through the figures I make. When I observe others, I see them through a lens of my memories, my history, and my cultures. We all believe what we see. Filtering through those memories and images, I become aware of connections with my personal history, my cultural heritage, and the present. I try to find a place that exists between the individual and his or her background. My figures are created in that place where memories and cultural histories come together. In the process of developing pieces, I continue to search for the truth of what we really look like and who we are.

**Akio Takamori,
*Dwarf and Girl
with Ball*, 2000**
Left: 27 x 19 x 14 in.
(68.6 x 48.3 x 35.6 cm);
right: 34 x 13 x 8 in.
(86.4 x 33 x 20.3 cm)
Coil-built stoneware;
electric fired in oxidation, cone 3–4;
underglaze
PHOTO BY ARTIST

Akio Takamori,
Boat (installation view), 2001
Tallest: 38 in. (96.5 cm)
Coil-built stoneware;
electric fired in oxi-
dation, cone 3–4;
underglaze
PHOTO BY ARTIST

Akio Takamori,
Ensemble (installa-
tion view), **2000**
Largest: 39 x 11 x 8 in.
(99.1 x 27.9 x 20.3 cm)
Coil-built
stoneware; electric
fired in oxidation,
cone 3–4;
underglaze
PHOTO BY ARTIST

I first sketch ideas from photographs, memories, and historical images. I look at many types of human images. I like the clay figures from ancient history, especially the Han and Tan dynasties in China. The compositions in Asian hand scrolls intrigue my imagination. I also refer to iconic images and paintings in the European tradition. To me, even anonymous people provide details that make me curious to examine each individual's inner life. A person can be royalty or a peasant, a leader or a servant—no matter how powerful or how humble, each person has a story and a place in history.

Next, I develop multiple working sketches that show measurements and proportions. By the time I begin building the form, I know how many inches each part should be. I use a sturdy sculpture clay body with large-particle grog, which helps minimize warping and cracking. This type of clay body also allows for rapid construction; I can build up to 2 feet (61 cm) at a time. When fired, the clay is buff colored, which provides an amiable and warm background to paint.

I use 1-inch (2.5 cm) coils to build the hollow figures. For stability, the walls are thickest at the bottom. I blend the coils as I build upward, and the walls become gradually thinner. The initial forms are less articulated, and I emphasize volume in the figures by pushing out from the inside. This technique creates fullness and roundness without compromising structural integrity. Small pieces of clay are added to the

Ceramics is often process-oriented, but I have simplified my methods to focus on larger ideas. The forms are uncomplicated. The poses are subdued. I choose certain methods of construction, firing, and surface drawing for consistency and predictability. I like the directness of this process, because then I can put the most effort into the conceptual development. I try to think about conventions, and then break out of them.

I try to think about conventions, and then break out of them.

outside features so that the walls aren't too thin. I use a plastic rib to smooth the sand from the surface. I leave few individual markings, in order to let the brushwork communicate ideas.

Once the piece is completely dry, I can begin the surface painting. The technique is an accumulation of washes of color. I use watered-down commercial underglazes, which I treat like watercolors. The ratio of underglaze to water varies, depending on the intensity of the color I want, but a good starting point is a 60:40 ratio. I start with a light wash to sketch the basic design, then add multiple layers of wash to create different depths and intensities of color. I prefer using thick, round watercolor brushes that hold a lot of liquid. I also use Oriental *smui* brushes and even a compact powder makeup brush to create effects. With each type of brush used, the line can be controlled or runny. On very small details or facial features, I use a thinner, more pointed brush, but on other parts I use a fat, round brush to let the colors run and drip.

I find the surface drawing the most satisfying part of the process. I seek a looseness with the brushwork that I don't find in constructing the form. There is a constant push and pull between controlled and less controlled, between deliberate and spontaneous. I stand back many times from the piece and look at drawings and photographs again. I continue to develop how I interpret the image and my memory of the image. I try to really look at the piece and contemplate how the surface can best capture the idea.

Once the surface painting feels nearly complete, I fire the pieces to cone 3–4 in an electric kiln (in an oxidation atmosphere). After the first firing, I add more washes of underglaze, because some colors have burned out. I fire a second time. I'll do multiple firings, with additional washes to intensify or mute colors, until I'm satisfied with the final coloration of the piece.

The clay figures, like people, don't exist in isolation. They interact with each other and with the environment, so the arrangement of figures is an important

Akio Takamori,
Sleeping Woman in Checkered Shirt
(detail), 2004
27 x 11 x 7 in
(68.6 x 27.9 x 17.8 cm)
Coil-built stoneware; electric fired in oxidation, cone 3–4; underglaze
PHOTO BY ARTIST

Akio Takamori,
Noble Woman and Court Woman, **2003**
Noble woman:
45 x 20 x 14
(1.1 x .51 x .36 m);
court woman:
46 x 21 x 11 in.
(1.2 x .53 x .28 m)
Coil-built stoneware; electric fired in oxidation, cone 3–4; underglaze
PHOTO BY ARTIST

Akio Takamori, *Empress and Queen*, **2003**
Left: 53 x 23 x 17 in. (1.4 x .58 x .43 m);
right: 42 x 32 x 17 in. (1.1 x .81 x .43 m)
Coil-built stoneware; electric fired in oxidation, cone 3–4; underglaze
PHOTO BY ARTIST

aspect of what I try to articulate. There is an optimal viewing height, but placement can also be symbolic of the heroic or the anonymous. Grouping creates tension between pieces, as a commentary of historical or cultural observations and assumptions. One piece alone may not manifest what I'm going after. In this project I'm making just one piece, one in which the Spanish queen Mariana (as painted by Velázquez) is dressed in black. She represents Western civilization and is meant to be juxtaposed to a Hang Dynasty court woman, as shown in the photo on page 147. Both women are exaggerated in form, perhaps to represent power, but each has a distinctive way to portray herself.

I'm influenced and intrigued by many different types of human images and objects. I wonder about the details of those lives. I wonder how many of those details would change if that person lived in a different time or a different culture. And how many of them would stay the same? I try to push past assumptions, and I don't stop until the piece is complete. It's important to trust yourself and not give up when you're looking for your own inspiration. It's easier to listen to skepticism and never finish a project, but seeing things to the end is a valuable experience. Pushing boundaries and being curious increase knowledge of the varieties of techniques and tools. This knowledge is necessary to find out what technique gives the desired effect. Get into the studio and stick with it. Something interesting will always emerge.

TECHNIQUE: COIL+FORM

Akio Takamori, *Queen* (detail), 2004

PHOTO BY VICKY TAKAMORI

1 Sketch of ideas and measured proportions. It's important to obtain accurate measurements so that the figure will be scaled correctly. Many sketches are done before the construction of the piece.

2 Beginning the coiling process. I use 1- to 1¹/₂-inch-thick (2.5 to 3.8 cm) strips of clay and build directly on a throwing bat that stays on a banding wheel.

3 To maintain even thickness in the walls, I blend the coils upward and downward rather than pinching the strips together. As the figure grows upward, the coils become progressively thinner in order to maintain structural stability.

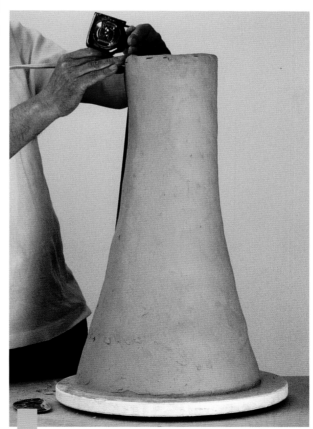

4 Smoothing the walls with a plastic rib and determining the position of the waist by measuring the proportions to the drawings.

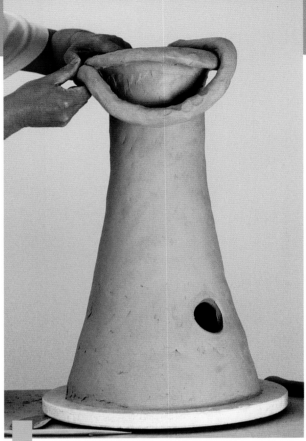

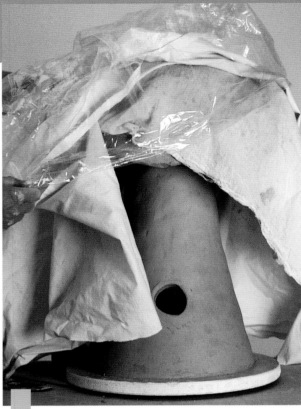

7 At the end of the day, I cover the form with cotton rags and wrap it with plastic sheets.

5 Forming the torso and skirt. Two holes are created to balance heat and moisture both inside and outside the structure.

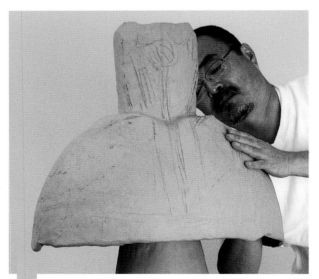

8 Simultaneously forming the torso and skirt. Volume and a sense of fullness are created by initially building a narrower structure, then pushing the clay out from the inside with a rib. The scratched lines serve as construction guidelines and are removed when they're no longer needed.

6 Developing the skirt by coiling it downward.

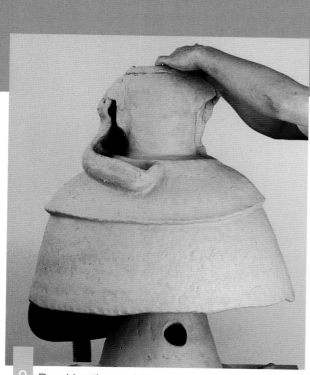

9 Reaching the neckline and creating the arms and sleeves in a resting position

11 Scoring and attaching wetter clay to the drier skirt form

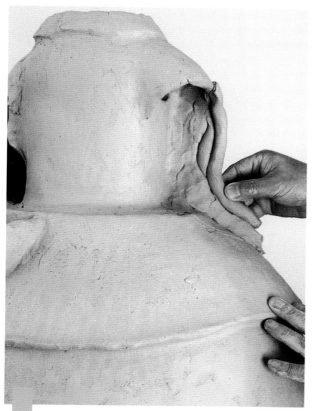

10 Continuing the arm construction

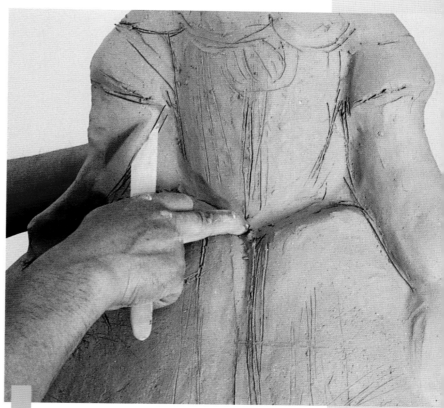

12 Adding thin strips of clay to refine and enhance the three-dimensional form of the dress

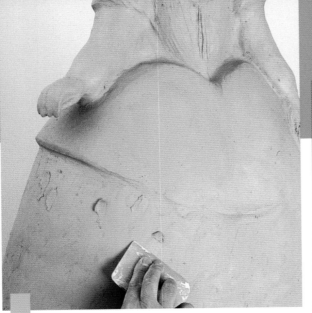

13 Smoothing the grog surface with a rib. Separately formed solid hands are attached to the figure.

14 Closing the hollow form with a clay plug

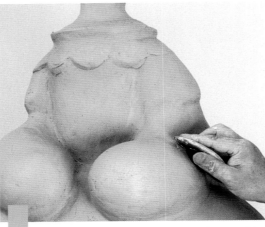

15 Finishing the surface and removing markings on the clay. To enrich the figure, the exaggerated sleeve form continues to the back.

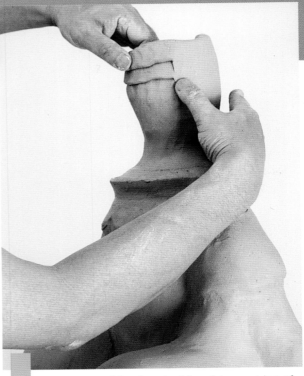

16 Continuing to blend and adding thinner strips of clay to form the basic head structure

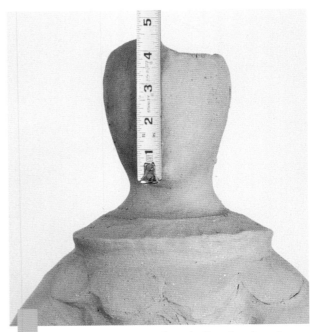

17 Measuring the proportions to the drawings to maintain an accurate representation of the original idea. I constantly refer back to the scale drawings to ensure that the figure's individual parts are consistent with the images and the figure as a whole.

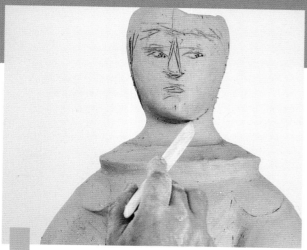

18 Delineating basic facial features with a wooden carving tool

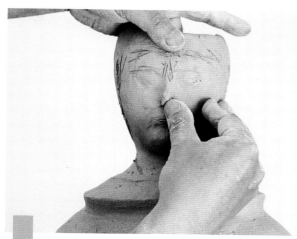

19 Using the carved features as guidelines, clay is added to create the three-dimensional features on the face.

20 Adding clay for the hairdo structure

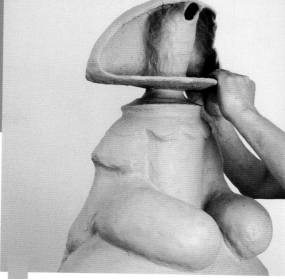

21 Building the hairdo around the cylindrical head structure; the cylinder lends stability to the large hair form. My timing of the construction of this form is based on the fact that the form's strength increases as it dries.

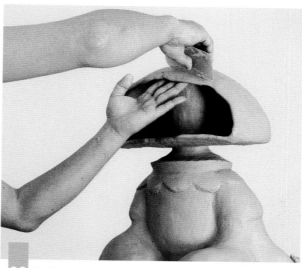

22 Further developing the hairdo with thinner coils and pushing out the form

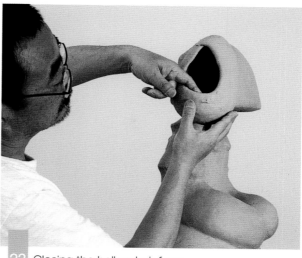

23 Closing the hollow hair form

AKIO TAKAMORI

24 Removing markings and smoothing the clay

25 Comparing the proportions of the figure to the drawings. At this stage I add clay to individual parts to refine and emphasize certain details.

26 Backside view

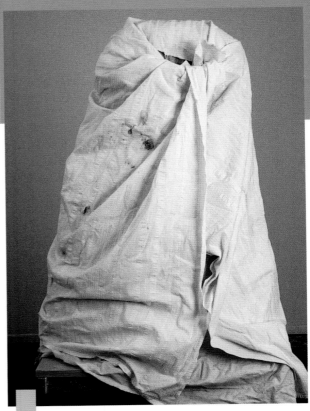

27 Wrapping the entire piece in cotton cloth for slow, even drying

28 Roughly sketching in underlying lines onto the green ware surface with watered-down black underglaze

29 Shading and color add depth and clarity to the design. The piece is now bone-dry.

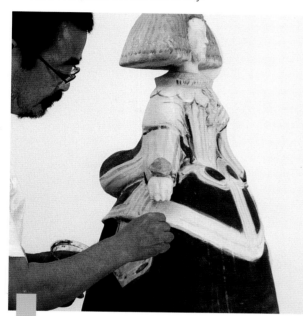

30 Adding a second layer of color to the underglaze wash

31 Profile view of the finished, unfired piece; facial expression was refined, and accents and further color were added as needed.

32 After the first firing (cone 4) in an electric kiln with an oxidation atmosphere. Some of the colors fade as the pigments burn out in the kiln and need further layers.

33 Further application of color and detail enhancement. The figure is fired again at a lower temperature (cone 3) in the electric kiln. It can be fired multiple times until the intensity of the colors and details becomes satisfactory.

**Akio
Takamori,**
Queen, 2004
32 x 23 x 13 in.
(81.3 x 58.4 x 33 cm)
**Coil-built
stoneware;
underglazes;
electric cone
3–4, oxidation**
PHOTO BY VICKY
TAKAMORI

GALLERY
OF INVITED ARTISTS

Claudia Fitch, *Chandelier with Milk Drops*, 2003
180 x 42 x 30 in. (4.6 x 1.1 x .76 m)
Slip-cast Dove White clay; cone 05; white glaze;
oil-based paint, gold leaf; aluminum frame,
brass attachments

PHOTO BY EDUARDO CALDERON

Sunkoo Yuh, *The Memory of Pikesville, TN*, 2003
34 x 29 x 26 in. (86.4 x 73.7 x 66 cm)
Hand-built porcelain; gas fired in oxidation, cone 10; glazes

PHOTO BY LARRY DEAN

Claudia Fitch, *Chinoiserie*, 1998
19 x 14 x 14 in. (48.3 x 35.6 x 35.6 cm)
Press-molded clay; Akio Stoneware; high-fire glazing

PHOTO BY ARTHER AUBREY

Jeffry Mitchell, *Three Elephants*, 2004
Base, 23½ in. (59.7 cm) in diameter
Ceramic, platinum

PHOTO BY AARON JOHANSON. COURTESY OF PULLIAM
DEFFENBAUGH GALLERY

Claire Cowie, *Still Life on Blue*, 2003
Installation: 4 x 4 x 12 ft. (1.2 x 1.2 x 3.7 m)
Ceramic mold-making materials:
Hydrocal plaster, latex, urethane, gesso;
unfired; watercolor and sumi ink washes
PHOTO BY STACEY HALPER

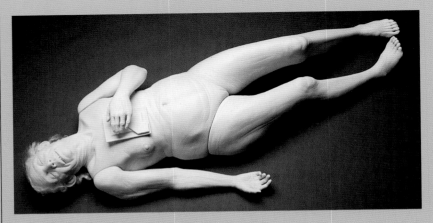

Tip Toland, *Rapture*, 2002
12 x 36 x 20 in. (30.5 x 91.4 x 50.8 cm)
Porcelain, sheep wool
PHOTO BY ARTIST. COURTESY OF NANCY MARGOLIS GALLERY

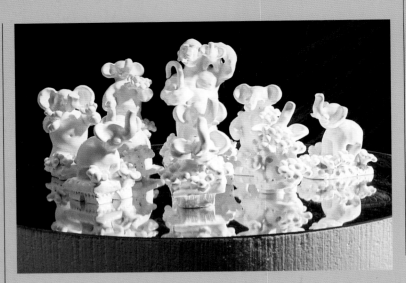

Jeffry Mitchell, *There's a Place for Us*, 2004
Tallest, 10 in. (25.4 cm)
Ceramic, polystyrene foam, acrylic stand
PHOTO BY AARON JOHANSON. COURTESY OF PULLIAM
DEFFENBAUGH GALLERY

Georges Jeanclos, *Kamakura*, c. 1988
12 x 24 x 12½ in. (30.5 x 61 x 31.8 cm)
Fired terra cotta
PHOTO BY ANTHONY CUÑHA. COURTESY OF FRANK LLOYD GALLERY
AND THE ESTATE OF GEORGES JEANCLOS

Tip Toland, *River of Patience,* **2002**
15 x 20 x 12 in. (38.1 x 50.8 x 30.5 cm)
Porcelain, synthetic hair, wax, paint
PHOTO BY ARTIST. COURTESY OF NANCY MARGOLIS GALLERY

Sunkoo Yuh, *Alfred Summer,* **2000**
96 x 42 x 30 in. (2.4 x 1.1 x .76 m)
Hand-built and cast stoneware; gas fired in
oxidation, cone 10; glazes
PHOTO BY LARRY DEAN. COLLECTION OF WORLD
CERAMIC EXPOSITION FOUNDATION, KOREA

Akio Takamori

Akio Takamori studied at Kansas City Art

Institute, receiving his BFA in 1976. He earned

his MFA from the New York State College of

Ceramics at Alfred University in 1978. His work

is represented in many public collections,

including the Carnegie Museum of Art, the Los

Angeles County Museum of Art, the American

Craft Museum, the Victoria and Albert Museum,

and the Taipei Fine Arts Museum. He was

awarded National

Endowment for the

Arts grants in 1986,

1988, and 1992. Mr.

Takamori is professor

of art in the Ceramics

Department at the

University of Washington. He lives in Seattle,

where he has a studio.

Michaelene Walsh
FIGURATIVE COMPONENTS

Michaelene Walsh,
Fetish Figure, **2001**
22 x 12 x 4 in.
(55.9 x 30.5 x 10.2 cm)
**Coil-built red earthenware; electric
fired, cone 05; glazes; plastic eyes,
rubber, steel wire**
PHOTO BY TOM NEFF

THROUGHOUT HISTORY, PEOPLE HAVE CREATED FIGURES FROM
clay. Some figures served specific cultural or spiritual functions, while others had personal or decorative value. Any figure—whether a common doll, a ceramic figurine, or a Roman statue—has a unique reason for being that places it in a specific location and time. Figures mirror and record the human experience, revealing aspects of both the inner and outer lives of those who made them. When we look at a figure we're asked to conjure up the circumstances surrounding its creation and existence. Commonly, figurative work reveals universal human emotions and experiences that transcend language and time. It is this subtlety of the figure in communicating human experience that's one of its most alluring qualities. As I work with soft clay, as those throughout history have, I respond to human gestures of sadness, mischief, joy, serenity, emptiness—a whole range of emotions. I attempt to recognize these qualities in the shape the material takes and to stop working when I find them strong and believable. Most of the time, the figures I create aren't planned. They emerge as my hands and subconscious mind work in tandem to find and respond to these emotional qualities. (It's as if I'm a conduit and the figure is the message.)

Michaelene Walsh, *Shadow of a Former Self*, 2004
39 x 20 x 5 in.
(99.1 x 50.8 x 12.7 cm)
Hand-built red earthenware using slab, coil, and pinch methods; electric fired, cone 05/04; low-fire slips and glazes

PHOTO BY TOM NEFF

I began my art career working with the figure because I was required to do so as part of a BFA curriculum. As I realized the emotional power and surprising psychological undertones possible in figurative work, I felt challenged to do more than that. I've always been interested in psychology, personality, character, and what lies below the level of our consciousness. Clay, as an expressive material, lent itself well to exploring such qualities. There's something inherent in clay that, when touched, allows a range of emotions to emerge. Early on I was captivated by clay's responsiveness to the creative process. Working with clay became tantamount to unearthing characters from the unnavigated place deep inside me, my subconscious. Figures with full emotional presence and seeming personalities emerged out of the material. I felt compelled to develop these characters and follow where they led me.

Much like the subconscious mind, a pliant lump of clay is full of unearthed potential. Loosely speaking, the best way to describe how I create a figure is to compare it to the process of drawing. In its raw state, clay is an ambiguous lump, ripe with possibility. Like a blank sheet of paper, it waits to be transformed. Both media are meditative and directly expressive. Wet clay is quite soft and malleable. It holds the impressions of fingerprints. As I pinch the clay, my fingertips, like pencil on paper, are making marks on the surface. These fingerprint traces on the form are important. And as in the act of drawing, the shape of the figure intuitively emerges out of the marks made by my fingers. A three-dimensional figure is "drawn" out of the clay.

There's something inherent in clay that, when touched, allows a range of emotions to emerge.

The techniques I use to construct my figures are simple and direct, using my hands and very few tools. Coiling and pinching, my main construction methods, are as elemental as clay itself. They derive from the innate way that any human being, given a lump of clay, instinctively forms it: literally pinching the clay

Michaelene Walsh, *Monkey Head Cup,* **2003**
5¹/₂ x 4 x 4 in. (14 x 10.2 x 10.2 cm)
Slab-built red earthenware; electric fired, cone 05; glazes
PHOTO BY ARTIST

into a shape or rolling out and pinching a shape from clay coils. Some small slab–building methods come into play when I want to make larger torso or leg forms, but I prefer the slow, rudimentary methods of coiling and pinching.

When making a figure, I spontaneously coil and pinch the wet clay into various hollow, globular forms. Eventually, many small "component" parts are created. I make these components at one sitting and keep them on the table in front of me on packing foam. The foam prevents the round forms from flattening out with gravity. As the components dry, I paddle and smooth them and connect them together into recognizable shapes, such as an arm, a head, or a leg. Then, while the component parts are still workable, at about leather-hard stage, I fabricate interlocking joints for each one, measuring to make sure the forms will fit after they're fired. Finally, I plan and cut holes in the backside of torso forms so that the whole figure may be hung on a wall. I apply slip or terra sigillata to each component, then bisque fire the still-separated pieces. Later, after the forms have been glazed and finished, I attach the parts with glue.

I use hollow component parts for several reasons. First, they're easily, directly, and quickly created, keeping that essence of drawing about them. Second, components are a manageable size to build, fire, store, glaze, and assemble with glue. Third, hollow parts are lightweight, so I can hang the final figure on a wall with just a few screws. Finally, small hollow components easily interlock with one another. This interlocking feature allows interchangeability of various parts throughout the process and is essential to how I build. Only later, after some play and consideration, do I glue them together into the larger whole that becomes the figure.

Working with component parts has another added benefit: it keeps the creative process mysterious and fresh from start to finish. I never make a maquette. The entire figure isn't actually put together until all its parts are finished and fired. This method of working leaves room for spontaneity. Before gluing, or even glazing or firing, I often change heads or limbs on a figure in response to something I see lying on the table in front of me. It's as if I'm drawing shapes, cutting them out and collaging them, and rearranging before I commit to the existence of the figure. Each sculpture is a sum of its components, but it often ends up being much more than just that. When this happens, I feel sure that I'm not really in control, and that keeps my art going.

I use clay red earthenware, a plastic, malleable clay made with a little grog, or sand, which assists in hand building and provides internal strength to the clay. Red earthenware fires to a low temperature, cone 05. I choose to work with this clay because it has a rich red-brown color that adds an undertone to all glazes and slips, giving a lustrous depth to its surface. Also, earthenware clay has historical associations with the "common man"; it's not considered an elevated material. So, in addition to its great physical properties, I find that earthenware's humble qualities fit well with the content of my work.

Michaelene Walsh, *Lost,* 2004
22 x 10 x 4 in. (55.9 x 25.4 x 10.2 cm)
Hand-built red earthenware using slab, coil, and pinch methods; electric fired, cone 05/04; low-fire slips and glazes
PHOTO BY TOM NEFF

I use three main surface treatments: slip, terra sigillata, and glaze. I rarely apply any raised texture to the body parts, so I look to surface treatments to add depth, texture, and color to the forms. Most of the surfaces in my work exist because they've been multi-fired, using any or all of these kinds of surfaces in undifferentiated layers. I fire pieces over and over, with little consideration for what, by strict ceramic standards, should or shouldn't work. I break the rules. I may put slip over glaze, or terra sigillata over glaze, in layers. I like the element of surprise when opening the kiln. My rule of thumb is that if I'm not satisfied with what came out of the kiln, I'll refire the work until I am.

There are a few challenges in this assembly-type work but also many benefits. Many component parts means many small objects to handle. I use *tons* of tiny stilts to

glaze pieces all around, and it takes time to load and unload kilns. Often I have many parts to work with, but no successful figure can be collaged from them. Occasionally, due to clay shrinkage or breakage, the fired, interlocking joints won't fit together. The parts may not "fit" together aesthetically, either, or a beautiful surface may go to the trash due to poor formal quality. The process of gluing component body parts together in just the right order can be time consuming, messy, and difficult. My figures hang on the wall, so I have to consider the overall weight of the piece; sometimes the combined weight of all the parts is too heavy to hang. On the flip side, using multiple parts means multiple choices in assembling the figure. Sometimes I can't make a decision! Also, small parts can be "approximately" remade if they break at any point in the process. When glaze and color are applied in a nonuniform way, such parts are more easily interchanged. These conditions allow me the creative freedom to make last-minute decisions and changes in the overall makeup of the figure.

In looking at others' figurative sculptural work, I find connections to my own. This lineage makes me curious about the power of the figure as sculpture and compels me to continue to explore it further as subject matter. I've found that making figures intuitively reveals parts of my emotional life that may be unconscious or underground. Ambiguous and expressive, clay is a perfectly direct material to explore such unknowns. It's one material that can be specific to the imagination, since fingers shape it. The figures I create are often unplanned; they emerge, like drawings, from my hands. They possess a certain identifiable emotional "character," at times sad, tragic, scary, funny, or a mix of feelings, but mostly, each is a sum of my observations of the state of the universal human psyche in this day and age. Looking at any sculpture of a figure made at any given point in time conjures up the circumstances surrounding its creation and existence. It is this ability of the figure to raise questions about the time frame in which I live, and to reveal some of its human concerns, that keeps me at work.

TECHNIQUE: COIL + PINCH

Michaelene Walsh,
Red Handed (detail), 2004

PHOTO BY TOM NEFF

2 Pinching a hollow head form

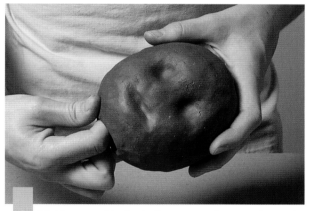

3 Making small indents for eye sockets and mouth

1 I don't need much space to work, but I like to keep sketches pinned to a nearby wall.

4 Using a dowel from the inside of the head to push out facial features and hair

5 Using my fingernail to draw the outline of an eye

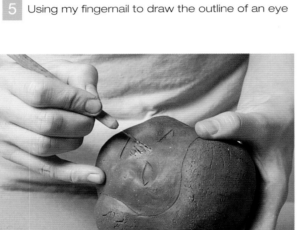

6 Scoring the slip in the area where the nose will be attached

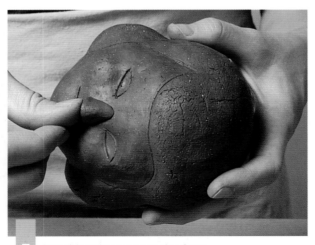

7 Attaching the nose to the face

8 Constructing the figure's torso using a hollow cylinder as a starting point. The cylinder is made from a ¼-inch (6 mm) flat slab of clay wrapped into a cylinder shape.

9 Pressing the soft clay out from the inside with my fingers to create the beginnings of the shoulders

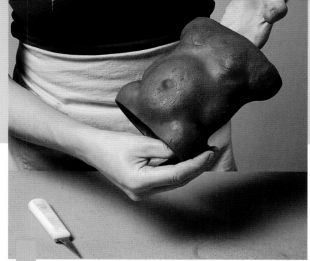

10 Pressing out from the inside of the torso form to create greater definition in the chest, stomach, hips, etc.

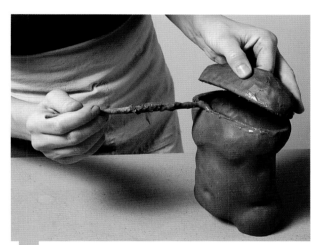

11 Attaching the shoulders to the torso form at the leather-hard stage. I score the areas being connected, then apply slip to each area.

12 Attaching leather-hard, pinched half-spheres to the bottom of the torso form. These create the hip and upper thigh areas on the bottom edge of the torso.

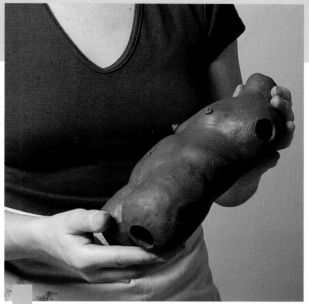

13 Holes are cut out of the torso form so that limbs can be attached later, after the firings, with a strong two-part epoxy. I usually cut the diameters of the holes in the torso a bit larger than the parts that will eventually be inserted into them. The larger holes allow wiggle room for glue and also allow for body parts to be interchangeable on all my figures.

14 A dowel is used to roll out a short, tapered form that will become an arm or a leg.

15 Finishing a leg form by pinching the clay

16 The coil-built form is closed up with a little pad of clay, enclosing air inside it. Paddling hollow, enclosed forms helps to smooth and shape them. The trapped air makes the form act like a balloon and keeps it from deflating as I paddle and work it into any shape: tapered, bulbous, or perfectly round.

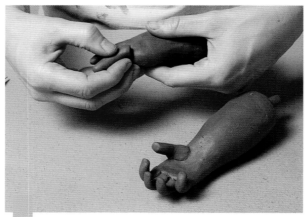

17 Securely applying fingers to the hand using the slipping and scoring method

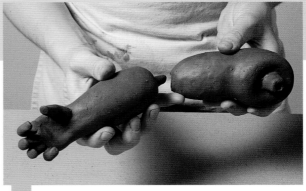

18 Checking the attachment of the upper arm to the lower one. The two portions of the arm are built so that they'll fit one another and can be easily glued together later; the fitting is created by placing a small plug onto one end of a limb. The plug acts as a firm, internal connecting device between parts.

19 Shaping the leg. The leg is begun in the same way as an arm, then the shape is roughly pinched out. All of the parts of my figures are as hollow and as evenly constructed as I can get them so that they'll be lightweight for wall hanging.

20 Finishing the lower leg as a boot form

21 Checking the connection between the upper thigh and lower leg. This connection will eventually be glued in place after all the firings, so it's important to check now that the parts fit together. The fit can't be easily altered after the firing. Light scoring on the plug will help the epoxy bind better to the clay surface.

22 The whole figure in mock assembly

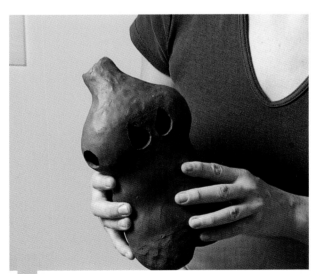

23 Teardrop-shaped holes cut in the back of the figure for hanging.

24 Brushing slip onto the torso form before bisquing it

25 Dipping a leg form in slip to add layers and depth to the surface

26 Loading the bisque kiln with various body parts

LOW-FIRE GLAZES
Tar Black

Matte black with mottled shiny specks. Fire to cone 07–01.

Gerstley borate	23
Borax	30
Flint	8.5
Iron chromate	13
Rutile	8.5
Cobalt oxide	8.5
Copper oxide	8.5
Total	**100**

Soft Sparkle

Just like the name sounds, it's beautiful over colored slips. Fire to cone 05.

Borax	21.9
Strontium	21.9
Soda ash	21.9
Whiting	21.9
Lithium	12.3
Total	**99.9**

Milk Base

Satiny white; opaque when thick. Fire to cone 05.

Ferro frit 3124	77.2
Kona F-4	13.9
Whiting	5.9
EPK	1.9
CMC	1
Total	**99.9**

Shiny Fat KP Blue

Shiny and opaque; takes stains excellently. Fire to cone 05.

Ferro frit 3124	80.2
EPK	9.4
Flint	9.4
Bentonite	.9
Total	**99.9**
Add	
blue stain	6

Santa Fe Slip for Low Fire

A no-rules-apply glaze-slip; I use it everywhere and at any stage: wet, bone dry, bisque fired, etc. Takes color well; use 2 to 5 tablespoons (20–40 g) per cup (300 g). Fire to cone 05.

EPK	50 g
Ball clay	50 g
Flint	50 g
Frit 3124	40 g
Zircopax	20 g

27 Glazing process: applying a thin wash of black copper oxide to the surface of the bisqued torso

LOW-FIRE CLAYS
Basic Red Hand-Building Clay

Fire to cone 04–01.

Redart	27.2 kg
Hawthorn Bond	13.6 kg
Ball clay	6.8 kg
Goldart	6.8 kg
Talc	9.1 kg
Grog, mixed mesh	1.4–4.5 kg
Barium	300 g

Anna's Black Clay

Fire to cone 04.

Goldart	10
Hawthorn	10
Redart	45
Barnard Blackbird clay	25
Frit 3124	10
Total	**100**

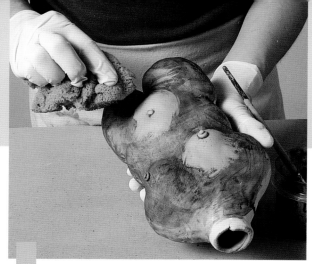

28 Wiping back the copper to create mottling and detail on the torso form

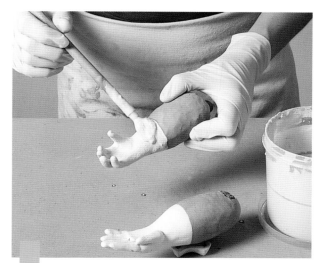

29 Applying cone 05 glaze to the hands. To prevent them from sticking to the kiln shelf, the hands will be fired on stilts.

30 Applying two coats of glaze to the head

31 Opening the kiln after completion of a cone 05 glaze firing

32 Laying out possibilities for assembling the figure

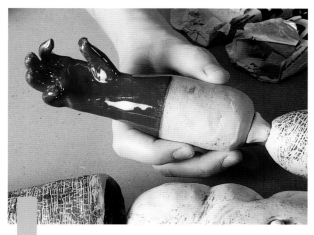

33 Epoxy cements a hand permanently in place.

Michaelene Walsh, *Red Handed*, 2004
21 x 9 x 4 in. (53.3 x 22.9 x 10.2 cm)
Coiled and pinched earthenware; electric fired, cone 05;
terra sigillata, glazes; plastic eyes, epoxy

PHOTO BY TOM NEFF

GALLERY
OF INVITED ARTISTS

Cristina Cordova,
La Huida, 2003
3 ft. (91.4 cm) tall
Earthenware; electric fired;
formulated and commercial
glazes, resin, acid, wire.
PHOTO BY SEAN BUSHER

Cristina Cordova, *Los Que Te Pienson*, 2004
12 x 13 in. (30.5 x 33 cm)
Earthenware; electric fired; formulated and
commercial glazes, resin, acid
PHOTO BY TOM MILLS

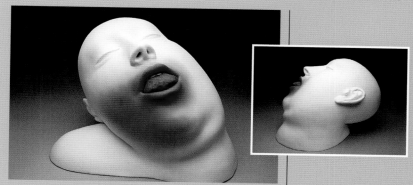

Tanya Batura, *Intricacies of Dreaming #1*, 2004
9 x 14 x 11 in. (22.9 x 35.6 x 27.9 cm)
Coil-built terra cotta; electric fired, cone 06;
acrylic paint
PHOTO BY MARC DIGEROS

Ryan A. Berg, *Gay and Lovin' It*, 2002
4$\frac{1}{2}$ x 6 x 3 in. (11.4 x 15.2 x 7.6 cm)
Low-fire ceramic
PHOTO BY ARTIST

Stephen Fleming, Untitled, 1998
11 x 8 x 7 in. (27.9 x 20.3 x 17.8 cm)
Pinched white earthenware; cone 1;
terra sigillata, cone 018
PHOTO BY ARTIST

Casey O'Connor,
Vessel Minded (Pot Head), 1999
18 x 8 x 8 in. (45.7 x 20.3 x 20.3 cm)
Porcelain slip-saturated plush animal and child's
sweater, wheel-thrown stoneware; salt fired, cone 11
PHOTO BY ARTIST

Cynthia Consentino,
Wolf Girl II, 2003
44^1/$_2$ x 23 x 19 in. (1.1 x .58 x .48 m)
Coil-built white earthenware; electric fired, cone 04;
terra sigillata, oils, cold wax finish
PHOTO BY JOHN POLAK

Andy Nasisse, *Orange Face Cup*, 2004
6 x 4 x 7 in. (15.2 x 10.2 x 17.8 cm)
Thrown and hand-built medium-temperature whiteware;
electric fired, cone 02; overglaze, cone 08
PHOTO BY WALKER MONTGOMERY

Lisa Clague, *Monkey Business*, 2004
85 x 32 x 24 in. (215.9 x 81.3 x 61 cm)
**Coil-built low-fire sculpture body and
low-fire earthenware; cone 05; mixed
media, metal, fabric, glaze, wax**
PHOTO BY TOM MILLS

**Ryan A. Berg, *Punky Centaur
(from Angel Finger)*, 2001**
36 x 27 x 12 in. (91.4 x 68.6 x 30.5 cm)
Low-fire ceramic; paper, light, fur
PHOTO BY ARTIST

Michaelene (Mikey) Walsh received her
BFA in crafts from the University of Illinois in
Urbana-Champaign and her MFA in ceramics
from the New York State College of Ceramics
at Alfred University. She has taught at various
academic and alternative institutions such as
the University of Georgia, Massachusetts
College of Art, Haystack School of Crafts,
Virginia Commonwealth University, Santa Fe
Clay, and the University of Washington.

Ms. Walsh has lectured and exhibited extensively across the United States. Recent shows
include "Gigantic" at the
Kirkland Arts Center in
Washington state and
"TransMissions" at the
Macon County Museum of
Art in Georgia. An upcoming
solo show of her work will
be held at the Seattle
gallery Grover Thurston,
which represents her. She is
currently assistant professor of art at Louisiana
State University in Baton Rouge.

Contributors

Index

Nick Park
Library & Learning Centre
Tel: 01772 225304

PRESTON COLLEGE

Please return or renew on or before the date shown below.
Fines will be charged on overdue items.

2 2 MAY 2008	− 1 FEB 2010	
0 8 JUN 2008	− 8 FEB 2010	
0 5 JUN 2008	1 5 NOV 2010	
	3 0 MAR 2010	
	2 7 FEB 2012	
2 2 OCT 2008		
− 8 JAN 2009	1 6 APR 2012	
2 3 FEB 2009	− 4 DEC 2012	
0 3 APR 2009	− 5 DEC 2012	
2 3 APR 2009		
0 2 JUN 2009		

Class   738. 82 .   D

Barcode   090717

30-PF-0806-PW-001